Pedagogies *of* Praxis

Pedagogies *of* Praxis

Course-Based Action Research in the Social Sciences

Edited by

Nila Ginger Hofman
Howard Rosing
DePaul University

ANKER PUBLISHING COMPANY, INC.
Bolton, Massachusetts

Pedagogies of Praxis
Course-Based Action Research in the Social Sciences

ISBN 978-1-933371-09-2

Composition by Jessica Holland
Cover design by Dutton & Sherman Design

Anker Publishing Company, Inc.
563 Main Street
P.O. Box 249
Bolton, MA 01740-0249 USA

www.ankerpub.com

Library of Congress Cataloging-in-Publication Data

Pedagogies of praxis : course-based action research in the social sciences / edited by Nila Ginger Hofman, Howard Rosing.
    p. cm.
Includes bibliographical references and index.
ISBN 978-1-933371-09-2
1. Action research. 2. Social sciences—Research. 3. Social sciences—Study and teaching. I. Hofman, Nila Ginger, 1962- II. Rosing, Howard.

H62.P3244 2007
300.72—dc22
                        2006034017

ABOUT THE AUTHORS

The Editors

Nila Ginger Hofman is assistant professor of anthropology at DePaul University in Chicago, Illinois. She has been teaching and conducting research amongst hidden urban populations in Chicago and in Zagreb, Croatia. She is the author of *Renewed Survival: Jewish Community Life in Croatia* (Lexington Books, 2006) and a number of articles that record the lives of hidden populations including undocumented immigrants and injection drug users in Chicago.

Howard Rosing is an anthropologist and executive director of the Steans Center for Community-based Service Learning at DePaul University in Chicago, Illinois. He has conducted research on issues of food access in the Dominican Republic and the United States.

The Contributors

Jess Paul Ambiee is a student in the University of South Florida's M.A. program in applied anthropology.

Joan Arches is associate professor in community planning and human services and the coordinator of the Youth Work Concentration at the College of Public and Community Service at the University of Massachusetts–Boston. She is the 2005 recipient of the University of Massachusetts President's Award for Public Service. She has been engaged in numerous service-learning and participatory action research (PAR) projects at the University of Massachusetts. Connecting her work with PAR initiatives internationally, she was a visiting professor at

DeMontfort University, in the United Kingdom, where she conducted research on community-university partnerships and low-income youth.

Irene Clare Beck is adjunct professor in the women's and gender studies program at DePaul University. Her areas of interest include gender equity, sexual harassment prevention, youth, and life narratives research. She has collaborated with Beth Catlett on several course-based PAR projects. These endeavors led to their founding the Women and Gender Research Initiative, which promotes community-based studies in the areas of gender, oppression, and resilience.

Sam Beck is an anthropologist and the director of the Urban Semester Program in New York City of Cornell University. He is the author of *Manny Almeida's Ringside Lounge: The Cape Verdean Struggle for Their Neighborhood* (Gavea-Brown Publications, 1992) and the coeditor of *Ethnicity and Nationalism in Southeastern Europe* (University of Amsterdam, 1981). He has conducted research in many different locations, including Iran (among Turkish-speaking pastoral nomads), Germany (among former Yugoslav migrant workers), and New York City (among the Puerto Ricans of Spanish Harlem).

S. Elizabeth Bird is professor of anthropology at the University of South Florida. She is the author of *The Audience in Everyday Life: Living in a Media World* (Routledge, 2003), as well as two other books and more than 50 articles and reviews in the area of media anthropology, folklore, and popular culture.

Daniel Block is associate professor of geography and director of the Neighborhood Assistance Center at Chicago State University. He is a founding member of the Chicago Food Systems Collaborative, a multidisciplinary, multi-university, community-university partnership focusing on increasing food access to underserved Chicago-area communities.

Mark Bouman is professor of geography at Chicago State University where he has taught since 1984 and where he cofounded the

Neighborhood Assistance Center and the Calumet Environmental Resource Center.

Beth Skilken Catlett is assistant professor in the women's and gender studies program and teaches in the sociology department at DePaul University. Her areas of interest include diversity in families, violence in intimate relationships, men and masculinity, and qualitative research methodologies.

Winifred Curran is assistant professor of geography at DePaul University. She has published in a number of journals, including *Environment and Planning A* and *Urban Geography*. Her research interests include gentrification, issues of race and gender in the city, the changing economies of cities, and qualitative methodologies.

Harpreet Gill is an undergraduate student majoring in geography at DePaul University. She has worked at Near Northwest Neighborhood Network, a Chicago community development organization, and is currently a GIS intern for the City of Naperville, Illinois. She plans to pursue a graduate degree in urban planning.

Euan Hague is assistant professor of geography at DePaul University. He has published in a number of journals, including *Annals of the Association of American Geographers; Cultural Geographies; Gender, Place and Culture; Antipode;* and *Scottish Affairs*. His areas of specialization include cultural, political, and urban geography.

David Hall is a senior lecturer in applied sociology at the University of Liverpool in the United Kingdom. He has coauthored *Evaluation and Social Research* (Palgrave Macmillan, 2004) and *Practical Social Research* (Macmillan, 1996) with Irene Hall and written extensively on service-learning pedagogy. His interests include applied research methods and voluntary sector studies.

Irene Hall is a research fellow in the School of Sociology and Social Policy at the University of Liverpool. She has a background in community development studies and has worked on community development in the Welsh valleys. Together with David Hall, she is a researcher for a European Commission project on science shops.

James Kuzin is a student in the University of South Florida's M.A. program in applied anthropology.

TABLE *of* CONTENTS

INTRODUCTION

This book is about building public interest partnerships between institutions of higher education and local community-based organizations (CBOs). It is not a how-to guide, but rather a compilation of case studies that discuss the implications, successes, and failures of such partnerships. In particular, we seek to document the ways in which course-based action research (CBAR) within the social sciences functions as an effective resource for establishing and reinforcing partnerships among students, academic officers, and local communities. Students and faculty, guided through CBAR, learn how to develop advocacy strategies for marginalized communities through firsthand exposure to local-level politics and power imbalances in these communities.

We use CBAR as an umbrella term that encompasses a variety of community-focused research, including community-based research (CBR), community-focused experiential learning (EL), and participatory action research (PAR). What brings each of these research models within the scope of CBAR is an underlying commitment to engaging undergraduates, faculty, and local community partners in building intercommunity ties through the shared goal of improving the lives of members of marginalized communities.

Further, each of these models seeks to design research in collaboration with and ultimately *for* local community partners, as opposed to strictly student-centered research or research that aims merely to provide a descriptive account of local communities, along with a handful of normative conclusions that might be drawn therefrom. (Catlett and Beck discuss this distinction more fully in Chapter 2.) CBAR methods and practices—such as anthropological, feminist-informed, social work, geographical, or sociological—achieve this by connecting students with local-level politics and thereby deepening their concern for and participation in social justice. By emphasizing the use of fieldwork as part of the learning experience, CBAR projects complement the theoretical component of students' experiences and research skills. As a result, students are able to critically evaluate the social, political, and economic realities that shape the lives of their fellow residents. As educators, researchers, and activists, we believe that CBAR enables students to critically evaluate their sociopolitical surroundings.

Although different research methods are employed in CBAR projects, our ultimate goal is to work in close collaboration with community partners and to integrate pedagogy with praxis. Following Paulo Freire's (1970) ideas, we understand *praxis* to signify an integration of community-based research for the purpose of empowering community partners, their stakeholders, and our students. We take seriously the importance of instilling a critical pedagogy in order to subvert laissez-faire politics. Praxis, we point out, can take place only when theory and practice are integrated in particular cultural—that is, economic, political, and historical—contexts.

Our contributions detail the challenges we have faced in developing and sustaining various CBAR projects. Addressing specific CBAR-related experiences of students, faculty, and their supporting institutions, we discuss the ways in which local CBOs and their stakeholders can be affected, and empowered, through CBAR. We further discuss the benefits and challenges faced by academic officers in launching CBAR as a means of advancing their institution's commitment to maintaining community partnerships and expanding innovative pedagogies.

CBAR has a natural affinity with the social sciences, such as anthropology, geography, and sociology, in that it employs the specific research methodologies of these disciplines with the objective of implementing positive social change. However, many educators—anthropologists and sociologists, for example—do not take advantage of their discipline-specific practice for the purpose of engaging students in local-level politics. Educators have largely ignored the resources available to them through their institutions (service-learning programs, for example) or the resources of the communities in which their home institutions are located. Many social science departments across the United States, for example, continue to teach research methods and action research confined to classroom instruction. Although institutions of higher education are catching on to the merits of CBAR, not all provide support for CBAR endeavors or take innovative pedagogies as seriously as we do. Untenured faculty face many obstacles when designing CBAR due to the time commitment associated with CBAR and the fact that the fruits of their labor often go unrecognized in their home departments and institutions.

As the contributions to this volume demonstrate, CBAR programs of various stripes are rapidly developing in universities across the United States. However, they still lag somewhat behind their European counterparts, which have thrived for several decades, on limited funding, through research pedagogies such as the Science Shop (see Chapter 8) and Social Action (see Chapter 4).

The popularization of CBAR in the United States is related in part to the efforts to engage institutions of higher education as the promoters of civic responsibility and public service. While many universities acknowledge the need to become more engaged with their communities, many programs—particularly those labeled service-learning or experiential learning—tend to focus more on volunteerism or student-centered intellectualism than action research. Thus, many educators understand the objectives of service-learning or experiential learning as means for promoting a desire in students for lifelong learning, selflessness, and volunteerism.

Emphasizing *morality* such as religious or ideological morality, the service-learning and volunteerism model has been endorsed by President George W. Bush who has famously called on *all* Americans to commit at least 4,000 hours, or the equivalent of two years, to service over the course of their lives (Corporation for National and Community Service, 2002). As a result of Bush's call to service, more than 130,000 public and private elementary and secondary schools, home schools, and after-school programs around the country received copies of the *Students in Service to America Guidebook* (Corporation for National and Community Service), which seeks to enlist young people in serving their local communities in order to develop habits of civic participation, morality, and responsibility. Bush's campaign, the USA Freedom Corps, was developed after the terrorist attacks of September 11, 2001. Its objective is to cultivate, as the Bush administration put it, a culture of service, citizenship, and moral responsibility. Critics of Bush's call to service observe that it seeks to eliminate government responsibility for providing for the young (through decent education and after-school programs), the sick (through universal health care), the elderly (through affordable care), and those impoverished by social disasters like Hurricane Katrina, as well as America's crisis of un- and underemployment. Placing the responsibility for the care of local communities and needy individuals on charitable organizations and individual citizens instead of government agencies is in line with the neoconservative politics of the Bush administration.

The contributions to this volume embrace different ideals, which move beyond the promotion of morality to advocacy for community partners and the social issues that define their struggle. They do this by placing an emphasis on how our discipline-specific practice can advance social justice in collaboration with community partners. By incorporating the use of field-research methodologies and social action as part of the learning experience, these contributions analyze and evaluate the impact of CBAR on student learning, faculty teaching, and research, while documenting the social outcomes of CBAR projects on community partners and stakeholders.

CBAR therefore has dual aims. On the one hand, CBAR is envisioned as an educational experience in which students participate in a research activity that meets the needs of community-based organizations. In fact, the projects described herein all seek to connect students to issues of social justice and community empowerment. On the other hand, CBAR also seeks to empower community members and to connect the university to the community by inspiring institutions of higher education, faculty, and students to envision and engage in the implementation of positive social change for local community partners.

Because CBAR ultimately serves the interests of three different constituencies—students, faculty and their supporting institutions, and community partners and stakeholders—our projects are guided by a number of recurring themes, which document the ways in which we learn, teach, and strive for positive change in our local communities. The case studies in this volume address how CBAR may serve as a pedagogical tool for attuning students to the power of research by addressing the challenges and benefits of CBAR and by examining how to maximize the impact of student research on community partners. Towards this end, the contributing essays examine how student engagement in action research can serve as a way to think critically about implementing social change and the promotion of social justice. They do this by examining how to effectively teach and design CBAR programs, beginning by asking how student work can be rendered more visible and how CBAR projects can realistically move toward PAR.

These and other overlapping issues are engaged in a variety of ways in this volume. For example, by looking at how CBAR can best serve a university's commitment to a community partnership, these essays explore the type of institutional support needed to sustain CBAR endeavors. Our contributing essays offer suggestions on how the goals of community partners and institutions of higher education can best be integrated. We argue that the establishment of effective CBAR projects is necessary if universities are to embrace a genuine commitment to incorporating innovative pedagogies across the curriculum that will engage and empower students, while serving the needs of their community partners and other stakeholders.

CBAR: A Political Pedagogy?

The CBAR literature addresses three broad and overlapping issues. The first is the practical "how to" concerns of successfully building and executing CBAR projects. The literature on this theme provides an important resource for hands-on information on methodological tools and lessons learned from previous and existing CBAR projects. The second issue articulates the educational value of CBAR to students. The corresponding literature describes the pedagogical challenges faced by CBAR's key participants: faculty, students, and community partners. The third theme highlights the inherently political nature of CBAR by situating it in the context of societal power imbalances (e.g., between the university and community partners), the tenure and promotion policies of institutions of higher education, and the impact of CBAR vis-à-vis recent changes in social welfare policies.

Arguably the most significant contribution to the literature on the practical implications of implementing CBAR, and its educational value to students, is that of Strand, Marullo, Cutforth, Stoecker, and Donohue (2003) in *Community-Based Research and Higher Education*. These authors discuss the specifics of how to build community-based research into the curriculum, to structure student learning, and to "produce usable research for the community" (p.168). One of the strengths of this text is that its case studies span the social and behavioral sciences without proclaiming a single or fixed pedagogy. Similarly, we draw on multiple pedagogies and research methods, which render our contributions applicable to a variety of discipline-specific and interdisciplinary approaches.

The educational value of CBAR for students has generated discussion (Brydon-Miller, 2001; Freire, 1970; Schensul & Berg, 2004; Simonelli & Roberts, 1998). This is understandable because CBAR projects originate at institutions of higher education where student-centered learning has been given priority and practitioners often need to justify the integration of CBAR into the curriculum. The argument has been made that community-based research not only enhances discipline-specific learning (e.g., the acquisition of knowledge, together with lived and field research experience), but also teaches collaboration between students and community partners.

One of the most important educational benefits attributed to CBAR is that it motivates students to become passionate about social justice and to produce new—and challenge existing—knowledge. Johnston, Harkavy, Barg, Gerber, & Rulf (2004) have linked CBAR to students gaining a greater sense of social responsibility by increasing their level of civic engagement. Lewis (2004) demonstrates how CBAR encourages students to move beyond charitable solutions for resolving social inequality by becoming critical thinkers. Unlike research confined to abstractions or driven by academic interests, students in CBAR courses directly engage its social, political, and economic contexts.

Polanyi and Cockburn (2003) express concerns about power imbalances between the university and community partners by showing how these partnerships have "contributed to some [community] participants' sense of insecurity or alienation" (p. 16). A case in point is the scheduling of project meetings on university grounds. Polanyi and Cockburn observe that such meetings create added challenges to university-community partnerships. For example, they observe that university participants are often indifferent toward the location of the meeting, whereas community partners are burdened by the cost of transportation to such meetings, delays in honoraria checks, and the frequent visibility of a sign at the designated meeting location announcing "psychosocial research."

One respect in which CBAR is particularly problematic for university faculty is that the merits of CBAR often are not acknowledged in tenure and promotion decisions. In her effort to integrate applied research into a sociology course, Joyner (2003) emphasized the need for institutions of higher education to alter their tenure and promotion policies to consider the products of such courses as scholarship. She argues that the largest obstacle to socially relevant research is the "narrow definition of scholarship that pervades in higher education today" (Joyner, p. 17). Given the growing interest in institutionalizing CBAR (and particularly service-learning), arguments such as Joyner's will become increasingly difficult for upper-level administrators to ignore.

An emerging theme in the CBAR literature concerns scholars who seek to critically analyze CBAR's role in light of recent neoconservative politics in the U.S., which are systematically dismantling a number of long-standing social welfare policies. As Hyatt (2001) and Keene and Colligan (2004) have pointed out, university-based service-learning initiatives do not exist apart from the social policies that have invigorated public support for such programs. Hyatt links the service-learning movement to efforts to promote volunteerism and individual responsibility in light of government downsizing, reduction in social welfare spending, and the privatization of public resources. She points out that institutions of higher education are "players" in the production of "neoliberal citizens," who, when engaged in service-learning, become desensitized to the political nature of their actions. In this political environment, Hyatt observes that students become believers in self-help mantras—the notion that communities can rebuild themselves from within without government assistance. Notwithstanding her critique, Hyatt continues to advocate for service-learning and applied research in her courses as a means to guide students toward thinking critically about their role in CBAR.

Future research on CBAR must incorporate the broader political contexts of the subject matter in order to challenge students and other members of privileged institutions to critically analyze their role in the very politics that they purport to challenge. If these issues are not addressed, CBAR threatens to become absorbed into the hegemonic repertoire of marketing and public relations initiatives that universities employ in order to increase their endowments through enrollment and fundraising strategies. For community-based research to keep its political edge, university participants and community partners must develop projects that challenge the broad societal structures of inequality by focusing on the specific policies and institutions that each individual project confronts.

Organization of the Chapters

This book describes a number of overlapping subjects, approaches, and settings. For example, Chapters 2, 3, 4, and 7 describe case studies involving youth, and Chapters 3 and 7 employ visual documentation as a research strategy. It is no coincidence that DePaul University is the home institution for several of our contributors: Rosing; Catlett and Beck; Curran, Hague, and Gill; and Hofman. As Catlett and Beck point out in Chapter 2, DePaul's Vincentian mission is uniquely supportive of the growth and development of progressive CBAR projects. Block and Bouman make a similar observation about their home institution in Chapter 6, where they note that the geography department at Chicago State University has had a long-standing interest in promoting university-community partnerships. We hope the case studies collected herein will serve as examples for encouraging others to work with their own institutions in developing similar CBAR projects.

Other patterns in the CBAR projects described by our contributors include the qualitative approach (e.g., photo elicitation, participant observation, oral history documentation, and team ethnography) as well as the urban setting of many of our projects. Five case studies (the DePaul and Chicago State University cases) involve CBAR projects in and around the Chicago area—a city with a long history of community-based research. Further, almost all of the contributors live and work in large cities—New York City, Boston, and Liverpool—which provide fertile settings for CBAR topics such as displacement and gentrification (Chapter 5); food access, health, and safety (Chapters 1 and 6); and empowerment, leadership, and community building skills (Chapters 2, 3, and 4). Some of these projects—notably those described in Chapters 1,

5, and 6—employ quantitative research instruments.

Our case studies are organized around a number of recurring themes associated with the design, support, and implementation of CBAR and the lessons learned from CBAR. These themes are developed from the points of view of the authors, the students, and the partner communities. They are developed further in the context of an overarching attempt to understand how CBAR functions, for example, by employing asset- or need-based social action approaches or feminist-informed, service-learning, or PAR-driven methodologies. CBAR projects are designed to problematize the lived realities of urban communities and experience the power of reflection, participatory democracy, or student involvement with local politics. CBAR ultimately seeks to erase the community-university divide, empower community partners, and explore innovative pedagogies. We narrate the CBAR experience by describing the challenges of undergraduate, graduate student, and community partner involvement; the experience of developing worthwhile projects during a quarter, a semester, or longer time periods; and the development and ethical limitations of CBAR.

In Chapter 1 Howard Rosing examines how undergraduate community-based research enables students to think critically about social policies for improving access to food in neighborhoods that are underserved by the market-driven retail sector. Rosing's students, guided through an anthropological applied practice course, researched corner stores in Chicago's Austin neighborhood (on the far west side of the city) as part of a multiyear project to understand local provisioning patterns. Rosing demonstrates that by engaging in a CBAR project, students developed an understanding of the methodologies and ethical limitations of CBAR and anthropological applied practice while learning about issues of privilege that impact food access in neighborhoods such as Austin.

In Chapter 2 Beth Catlett and Irene Beck explore how faculty, students, and young community residents collaborated on a feminist-informed PAR project: "Teen Girls Re-Vision East Rogers Park." The authors describe how DePaul students compiled life narrative interviews with young teenage girls from low income families at Family Matters, a CBO in Chicago's Rogers Park neighborhood (on the far north side of the city) by employing an asset-based approach. The research project serves as a basis for addressing gender-related oppression, community development in an economically and racially diverse urban neighborhood, and women's empowerment. Catlett and Beck also illustrate the unique opportunities provided to them by both DePaul University and their department that enabled them to design and implement the CBAR project.

Sam Beck also explores CBAR with teens in Chapter 3, in which he describes how teenage boys from the Bedford-Stuyvesant (Bed-Sty) neighborhood in Brooklyn, New York, joined premed Cornell University students in an eight-week project called "Healthy Wednesdays in Our Hood." In order to better understand teens' needs and their lives in the built environment, Beck's project employed an asset-based approach to discourage the students from reproducing the mass-media-driven images and stereotypes of poor inner-city youths in dilapidated urban neighborhoods. Beck's asset-based approach involved asking the teens to document their experiences of their neighborhood by photographing "healthy places," writing captions for the photographs, and sharing those experiences with the students. As Beck explains, the collaborating partner viewed the CBAR project as a way to remove young men from the distractions of peers and street culture, and to encourage their academic interests and the development of alternative visions of the future. Challenging the assumption that the Bed-Sty kids should aspire to professional work, Beck points out that the project provided important insights into the construction of successful community service-learning and PAR work for all constituencies involved in the project (the community partner, the teens, and the students).

Continuing on the subject of CBAR with young people, Joan Arches illustrates in Chapter 4 how the Healthy Initiative Collaborative: Community-University Partnership (Hic Cup) served as a way to develop leadership, action research, and community building skills for low income, at-risk youths (ages 9–16). Embracing a need-based social action approach, undergraduate students met with Hic Cup youths on a weekly basis to help foster an understanding of the issues they face in their community and to ensure that their needs were being expressed. Arches points out that the teens, in collaboration with the undergraduates, were able to document their social needs as well as design and carry out a plan for social change. One of the realizations of the weekly meetings was the need for a basketball court in the community. Once the need was articulated, the youths engaged in petitioning, fundraising, proposal writing, community meetings, and other activities to make the basketball court a reality.

In Chapter 5 Winifred Curran, Euan Hague, and Harpreet Gill discuss students' experiences with the practical applications of an urban geography course. Working in a predominantly Hispanic residential area on Chicago's southwest side, undergraduate students generated a comprehensive building survey for Pilsen Alliance, a partner CBO that is seeking to forestall gentrification and the displacement of neighborhood residents. Students studied the social and political complexities of urban land use, zoning, and tax increment financing regulations, and collected historical and visual documentation of the area. The authors point out that community-focused experiential learning and reflection put students, faculty, and the community partner in touch with the practice of participatory democracy.

In Chapter 6 Daniel Block and Mark Bouman explore community-based learning at Chicago State University, where many students are working African-American mothers. Working through the Frederick Blum Neighborhood Assistance Center, an outreach center that provides research and information for local community groups, the authors describe how the collaborative CBAR projects they designed seek to erase the community-university divide as well as the boundaries between undergraduate and graduate student involvement. The authors address the inherent difficulties of working with nontraditional, graduate, and undergraduate students in community-based projects and discuss how these and other conflicts are negotiated in courses that advocate for student involvement in community-centered research experiences and local politics.

The last three chapters examine the effects of CBAR by examining the effectiveness of student-produced work, learning, and community-based partnerships. In Chapter 7, Elizabeth Bird, Jess Paul Ambiee, and James Kuzin describe the process of designing and implementing a CBAR partnership with Prodigy, a cultural art program that serves so-called at-risk youth. The authors discuss the social changes and student learning that occurred as a result of a semester-long CBAR project in a visual anthropology class. They address the specifics of developing the project and explore the challenge of community participation, team ethnography, and the completion of a meaningful project that is of value to the community partner. They emphasize the need for student reflection, faculty monitoring, and debriefing the community partner about every stage of the research.

In Chapter 8 David and Irene Hall describe Interchange, a participatory research initiative in Liverpool. Interchange brings CBOs together with faculty and sociology students from three universities in Liverpool. The authors describe how, by partnering with local CBOs, students gained research experiences that ultimately resulted in recommendations for policy change, program evaluation, and feasibility studies. They point out that the community partners have been able to use the student-produced reports in a variety of ways. A follow-up survey with students who have graduated from the program attests to the long-term impact of their experiences with Interchange and the transformative potential of CBAR for community partners. The authors also point out that gaining university support for these types of initiatives has not been easy and that funding has been limited. Although the results have been heartening at the local level and the work has received national and international recognition, they emphasize that CBAR is still regarded as a pioneering way to conduct research, teaching, and learning.

In Chapter 9 Nila Ginger Hofman examines the aftermath of CBAR in four CBOs in and around Chicago through a series of follow-up interviews with the CBO representatives. Emulating the case studies described in the foregoing chapters, the CBO representatives interviewed by Hofman include a small business development organization that combats gentrification, a community center that offers services ranging from citizenship preparation classes to emergency services, a youth organization that provides services such as literacy and job readiness training, and an organization that assists noncitizens in applying for immigration benefits. Hofman describes how students used action-oriented ethnographic data collection in all projects in order to suggest how CBOs can best serve their population and how the CBAR projects were designed in collaboration with the community partners. She offers a number of tentative conclusions about lessons learned from these projects, including that CBAR works best when fewer students conduct research at one particular organization, when contact is sought and maintained with *all* members of the participating CBOs, and when the different phases of students' research are communicated throughout the project with community partners.

References

Brydon-Miller, M. (2001). Education, research, and action: Theory and methods of participatory action research. In D. L. Tolman & M. Brydon-Miller (Eds.), *From subjects to subjectivities: A handbook of interpretive and participatory methods* (pp. 76–89). New York, NY: New York University Press.

Corporation for National and Community Service. (2002). *Students in service to America guidebook.* Washington, DC: Author.

Freire, P. (1970). *Pedagogy of the oppressed.* New York, NY: Continuum.

Hyatt, S. B. (2001, Spring). 'Service learning,' applied anthropology and the production of neoliberal citizens. *Anthropology in Action, 8*(1), 6–13.

Johnston, F. E., Harkavy, I., Barg, F., Gerber, D., & Rulf, J. (2004, Summer). The urban nutrition initiative: Bringing academically-based community service to the University of Pennsylvania's Department of Anthropology. *Michigan Journal of Community Service Learning, 10*(3), 100–106.

Joyner, L. M. (2003). Applied research in the pursuit of justice: Creating change in the community and the academy. *Social Justice, 30*(4), 5–20.

Keene, A. S., & Colligan, S. (2004, Summer). Service-learning and anthropology. *Michigan Journal of Community Service Learning, 10*(3), 5–15.

Lewis, T. L. (2004, January). Service learning for social change? Lessons from a liberal arts college. *Teaching Sociology, 32*(1), 94–108.

Polanyi, M., & Cockburn, L. (2003, Summer). Opportunities and pitfalls of community-based research: A case study. *Michigan Journal of Community Service Learning, 9*(3), 16–25.

Schensul, J. J., & Berg, M. (2004, Summer). Youth participatory action research: A transformative approach to service learning. *Michigan Journal of Community Service Learning, 10*(3), 76–88.

Simonelli, J., & Roberts, B. (1998, Fall). Connecting classroom with community: Service and professional socialization in applied programs for undergraduates. *Practicing Anthropology, 20*(4), 45–48.

Strand, K. J., Marullo, S., Cutforth, N., Stoecker, R., & Donohue, P. (2003). *Community-based research and higher education: Principles and practices.* San Francisco, CA: Jossey-Bass.

Food for More Than Thought: Course-Based Action Research on Corner Stores in Chicago

1

Howard Rosing

While at the stores I noticed that the employees and owners were extremely attentive to the actions of each customer in the store. I was constantly aware of being watched. On one occasion as I was leaving a store the owner wanted to know which way I was taking home, because he was concerned for my safety.[1]

—Undergraduate student researcher

This chapter examines the process of planning and teaching an undergraduate applied anthropology course using a critical pedagogical approach that incorporates community-based research on corner stores in the Austin neighborhood of Chicago. The research served as a means to inform and think critically about policy decision-making and grassroots efforts toward improving food access in a neighborhood that has long been underserved by the corporate retail food sector. Students were guided through research that was part of a university-community partnership called the Chicago Food Systems Collaborative (CFSC). The students' contributions to CFSC's multiyear research project were small, but offered insights that were unique and informative. They learned firsthand about applying ethnographic methods, the ethical limitations of applied practice, and how public policy, race, and class impact food access in neighborhoods such as Austin.

This chapter has four objectives. The first is to describe the context within which this research project took place. Chicago is a city currently undergoing significant physical and social transformation, including gentrification, that is, transforming many working class communities into affluent neighborhoods with an abundance of commercial and public services. On the periphery of such developments exist neighborhoods like Austin that lie just outside the core areas of so-called revitalization and

urban renewal projects. The second objective is to outline efforts at
DePaul University to engage students in community projects with nonprofit organizations in neighborhoods like Austin. The university has a
commitment to working in neighborhoods where underserved and
oppressed communities are seeking solutions to critical social issues. As
Catlett and Beck describe in Chapter 2, DePaul takes service seriously
and has in recent years supported institutionalizing service-learning in
the curriculum. The third objective is to describe a course, titled
"Community-Based Applied Practice," in which students conducted
research on corner stores in Austin. The fourth and final objective
explores the students' analyses of their data and, in particular, how these
analyses illuminated the everyday aspects of corner stores.

The Context of CBAR

Corner stores are a distinct part of urban neighborhoods in the United
States. In low-income neighborhoods of color, corner stores are frequently the sole source of food for residents marginalized by profit-driven supermarket chains that do not value their demographic as a target market. In
Chicago, where race and class divisions within and between neighborhoods are far from subtle, corner stores play an important role in urban
provisioning. This is especially true in predominantly African-American
neighborhoods, where segregation maintains a foothold and where gentrification has yet to advance its onslaught of investment in residential and
commercial development. Stores in these neighborhoods range from
mom-and-pop convenience stores to small grocers with minimal amounts
of fresh meats and produce. Some stores present the facade of a grocer,
although their contents lean more toward alcoholic beverages than food.
Some double as centers of neighborhood social life and turn into targets
of police surveillance. These constitute some of the so-called "hotspots" of
a city that can't seem to resolve long-standing concomitant crises in housing, employment, and education, but can spend millions of tax dollars on
video cameras to watch residents (Colias, 2005). Police cameras with
flashing blue lights warn those who choose to congregate at the store
entranceway that a gaze is upon them as if to say "you are not safe."

Safety is an expected characteristic of college campuses such as DePaul University, in the heart of Chicago's North Side. Blue lights on the campus shine through the night to identify safety phones, as if to say "we will keep you safe." Students in a class that I regularly teach off campus have repeatedly remarked how DePaul's main campus—embedded within the affluent neighborhood of Lincoln Park—is "like a bubble" that many of their peers rarely leave. Corner stores in low-income neighborhoods of the city sharply contrast with local food stores, cafes, and cafeterias run by the university that cater to the mass consumption of thousands of students. The sole corporate food service purchases food in bulk, offers great variety, charges students at significant margins via identification cards, and employs staff that is almost entirely of color. In contrast, the corner stores where my students conducted research bought food in small quantities, offered little variety, accepted only cash and government food aid cards, and typically did not hire the local, predominantly African-American residents. Indeed, as the student suggests in the opening quotation, some of the largely nonresident owners feared the community.

It is difficult to write about corner stores in Chicago without thinking about their distinct role in processes of social, economic, and racial inequality in the U.S. During the immediate aftermath of Hurricane Katrina in New Orleans in August, 2005, corner stores were the context for racialized media constructions of black and white Americans as looters and starving victims, respectively. In early 2006 this appears analogous to my white student in the opening quotation being perceived as someone who needed to be protected from the black neighborhood by the store owner. In the owner's mind the student was a potential victim rather than a prospective shoplifter. The student's comments captured the essence of racial tensions in Chicago and many U.S. cities. Such tensions come to life for the broader public during moments of social, economic, and political crises, such as natural disasters. But they are brewing in the subtle (and sometimes less than subtle) interactions between racially defined groups. Documenting these types of social interaction is the central focus of ethnographic inquiry.

Engaging in qualitative research in Chicago, including observation and in-depth interviews, poses a complex challenge for seasoned practitioners, let alone for relatively untrained undergraduate students. The city is ripe with social, economic, and political issues stemming from processes of deindustrialization, racial segregation, and a municipal development strategy focused on increasing the tax base by driving up property values in the city's urban core. Gentrification—a practice that seeks to attract affluent residents and commercial interests into neighborhoods previously abandoned by real estate developers—has been radically transforming the face of the city since the 1980s. Working-class neighborhoods have become targets of developers thirsty to sell young professionals an urban lifestyle combined with trouble-free access to goods and services. In the process historical patterns of segregation have shifted, resulting in the dismantlement of neighborhoods of color. Gentrification typically displaces longtime residents and transforms the aesthetic quality of the neighborhood. As Curran, Hague, and Gill describe in Chapter 5, one of the first neighborhoods to transform in this manner—from working-class and largely Puerto Rican to affluent and primarily white—was Lincoln Park, the host to DePaul.

Dispatching students into the city as ethnographers who are unfamiliar with these changing social dynamics requires a significant amount of planning and preparation. Most students at DePaul whom I have encountered are aware of gentrification but are unaware of its complexities. They don't often realize that what lies beneath the creation of gentrified neighborhoods is public policy. Students often express the idea that the primary impetus for neighborhood change is the real estate market rather than the enlistment of public resources on behalf of for-profit developers. They are sometimes surprised to learn about the sale of publicly owned land to developers at a discount and the use of eminent domain law to remove public (and sometimes private) housing. Also behind gentrification is the advance of generous tax incentives for residential and commercial developers to produce housing and retail shops that serve middle- and upper-class clientele and augment the municipal tax base.

The way students respond to learning about gentrification reflects their personal histories and identities. DePaul students come from a wide variety of backgrounds, but I have noticed a degree of polarization in how they understand gentrification. Those who struggle to pay private school tuition while maintaining full-time employment do not see themselves as part of gentrification processes by any means. Indeed, some of these students come from neighborhoods undergoing economic transformation. They are often not surprised by the fact that public policy does not enable low-income people to remain in their communities. Other students view these social issues as existing outside their immediate day-to-day world and relegate them to the problems of the so-called "inner city" or the "underprivileged" poor, whom they believe can be aided through community service. Gentrification, for many of these students, produces what some have referred to as "safe areas" and the Austin neighborhood lies clearly outside their safety zone.

Austin is situated at the very western boundary of Chicago in what is popularly referred to as the West Side. Since the 1960s forces of racial segregation shaped the neighborhood's demographics in a way common to many city neighborhoods. It was in neighborhoods such as Austin that lenders practiced redlining, or the act of drawing a red line around areas where they would not make loans as a means to maintain the racial make-up of a neighborhood (Pogge, 1992). Nonetheless, Austin was once a predominantly white neighborhood, but by the 2000 census it was 89.8% African American (Northern Illinois Planning Commission, n.d.). The neighborhood of 117,527 residents is the largest community area in Chicago. Furthermore, its location on the western border of the city removes it from the core neighborhoods under gentrification. Austin is nestled against the relatively affluent suburb of Oak Park. In recent years, this has resulted in gentrification trickling in from the west. Yet Austin has remained a working-class neighborhood with a median income of $33,663, as compared to $38,625 in Chicago generally and $59,183 in Oak Park (Northern Illinois Planning Commission).

Figure 1.1

Source: City of Chicago Department of Planning and Development, 2004

In spite of its size Austin is not a well-known neighborhood to most DePaul students. It is at least a 30-minute drive from campus, and most students are unlikely to have reason to venture into the neighborhood, although a few students volunteer at one or two of Austin's community organizations. Students are generally unaware of Austin's many important assets, the most important of which is a vibrant community life based on block clubs, churches, schools, libraries, community organizations, and activist groups (Choksi, 2004). During the warmer months there are out-door festivals, and people spend time building community gardens. A weekly farmers' market supports neighborhood growers and African-American farmers from central Illinois (Choksi, 2004).

If anything, most students are likely to have heard negative characteristics ascribed to the neighborhood. The mainstream media often equate Austin with high crime and regularly report on criminal activity as a West Side phenomenon with racial undertones that weave the neighborhood into a homogenous danger zone. Official police reports illustrate that crime is certainly a significant problem in the area, but it varies greatly from neighborhood to neighborhood (Chicago Police Department Research and Development Division, 2004). More important, given Austin's large geographic dimensions and population relative to other Chicago neighborhoods, police and media reports distort the reality of crime concentration within the neighborhood. As a result, students with little or no knowledge of the neighborhood are likely to arrive to class with negative and distorted views about it.

Aside from students who may be from Austin, most are unlikely to have ever engaged with any part of the neighborhood's commercial sector, let alone small food stores. Moreover, there are no well-known night clubs or restaurants that could draw students in large crowds, and most stores largely serve the interests of local residents rather than visitors or tourists. CBAR projects, therefore, often require faculty to guide students into unfamiliar spaces. For example, one student informed me that her first visit to Austin was one of the few times she had left Lincoln Park during her four years at DePaul. In her field notes, she reflected on her initial impressions of Austin's commercial sector:

> The storefronts were typically a little run down. Many of the storefronts had chipping paint or rusted iron/metal bars on the front of the windows and doors. They did not have a "clean" or well-maintained look on the exterior. The bars on the windows and doors also added to this.

As this quotation demonstrates, students involved in CBAR may initially focus on their preconceived understanding of a place (in this case, the West Side), which can result in reaffirming stereotypes. Ironically, during an in-class reflection this student later noted that she also observed storefronts and businesses that were very well maintained.

Course-Based Action Research at DePaul

The historical processes that led to racial disparities in U.S. cities can be ignored in DePaul classrooms, yet they are alive and well when students venture out into Chicago neighborhoods. Experiential learning—a strong initiative of the university—seeks to move students out of the classroom and into neighborhoods where they can engage with unfamiliar people and places. Community-based service-learning (CbSL), for example, encourages students not only to explore city life off campus but to perform service projects that reciprocally contribute to their learning experience and to the mission of community-based organizations. When critical analysis and reflective discussion is incorporated into such courses, students begin to understand the systemic reasons why certain people are mistreated, underserved, and oppressed.

One way to help boost critical understandings of social inequality is to devise projects that support faculty and are centered on the needs of the community instead of solely student focused. For example, the Steans Center for Community-based Service Learning at DePaul provides support to faculty, community organizations, and students. The mission of the center is to provide

> educational opportunities grounded in Vincentian community values to DePaul students. The Center seeks to develop mutually beneficial, reciprocal relationships with community organizations in order to develop a sense of social agency in our students through enrollment in CbSL courses, community internships and placements, and community-based student employment. (DePaul University, 2003b, ¶ 1)

The center has identified community-based research as a service-learning pedagogy that, when incorporated into courses, can serve the practical research interests of its community partners. CBAR, as we have termed such projects, is therefore an important way that the university practices its mission of service while guiding students to become critical thinkers and socially engaged members of society.

My involvement with CBAR at the Steans Center began during the fall of 2001 with collaboration between myself and Nila Ginger Hofman, a faculty member in the anthropology department. Hofman and I began to conceptualize how DePaul students in applied anthropology courses could offer research as a service to partner community agencies of the Steans Center. We devised several projects with multiple agencies, each with particular unrelated research interests. The pilot course, which occurred during the spring 2002 quarter, informed us how to move forward in future courses. We left the experience looking to hone our expectations of students and more narrowly define our research objectives. Eventually we would also limit the number of community partners linked to a particular course to one or two and find more user-friendly ways of disseminating reports to agencies than delivering a stack of individual student papers.

The following academic year community-based research was built into a new curriculum in anthropology that involved a series of applied courses, including an international applied anthropological practice course. Eventually anthropologists joined faculty from other social science departments (see Manley, Buffa, Dube, & Reed, 2006), and further collaboration with the Steans Center on developing CBAR projects began soon thereafter. The collection of disciplines offering CBAR widened to include sociology, anthropology, women's studies, and geography. The center now offers faculty consultation, site and project development, assistance with internal review board applications, and support in the form of paid research assistants.

The support given by DePaul University to CBAR projects led to student involvement in a variety of important research projects. These include researching community-level responses to private developers (as Curran, Hague, and Gill describe in Chapter 5), fraudulent immigration counseling services, food resources in proximity to public housing, support for the rights of day laborers, the role of remittances among Mexican immigrants, community residents, perspectives on economic development, and the empowerment of teen girls (which Catlett and Beck describe in Chapter 2). In each of these cases, DePaul faculty partnered with a community organization that sought to inform itself about a particular issue related to the people it served. The projects contained varying levels of participation by the community partner, but all were driven in the first instance by the interests of the organization.

Community-Based Applied Practice

Perhaps the most important lesson learned from consulting faculty about CBAR is that project goals should maintain low expectations for quantity but high expectations for quality. I first began to understand this principle while watching the outcome of Nila Ginger Hofman's course during the spring 2002 quarter. Drawing on Hofman's experience, I began to apply lessons learned to the planning of my own course, the first offering of community-based applied practice. That summer I read an article in a local newspaper about the Institute for Community Resource Development (ICRD), an organization that brought organic produce to the Austin neighborhood through urban farming and organizing a farmers' market. In October I met with ICRD's president, LaDonna Redmond, in an effort to explore ways that DePaul students could support the organization's work. Redmond was deeply involved in community organizing around food issues and is nationally known for her involvement with urban farming and activism on the West Side. She explained a multitude of projects in which ICRD is involved, and we discussed a variety of ways that DePaul students might add value to them.

Redmond wasn't interested in supporting academic research for the sole sake of improving someone's career. Austin, like many Chicago neighborhoods, had been the subject of study by university researchers who followed in the path of the renowned Chicago School of Sociology at the University of Chicago during the early part of the 20th century. Chicago School of Sociology researchers treated neighborhoods like Austin as laboratories for themselves and students. In quite the opposite fashion, Redmond informed me that she was part of organizing the Chicago Food Systems Collaborative (CFSC), a mix of community residents and university researchers who collected data in a participatory manner that served the interests of Austin's residents. Redmond's vision was to develop an alternative food system built on support for local organic farmers and employment of neighborhood residents. Social scientific research was a small part of her long-term goal of opening a community-supported grocery store.

The impetus for bringing more food options to Austin cannot be separated from processes of racial segregation in Chicago. Major supermarket chains did not view the neighborhood of 117,000 residents as a valuable target market. It wasn't until recently that a chain store opened on the far north border of Austin, but it was inaccessible for many neighborhood residents and especially those who depend on public transportation. Consequently, CFSC had the specific goal of documenting and mapping the current food resources in Austin, which were primarily small grocers.[2]

In November 2002 Redmond invited me to attend a CFSC meeting, after which I participated as a representative from DePaul. Since DePaul was not initially a part of the grant funding agreement, I remained an unfunded participant with the sole purpose of finding ways that DePaul students could support CFSC's ongoing work.[3] At the first meeting I learned that the principal investigator, Danny Block, was coordinating a market-basket survey to document food availability in the neighborhood. I also learned that one of CFSC's interests was to gain a deeper understanding of the role of the corner stores. I suggested that perhaps students from my applied anthropology course could conduct ethnographic research on small grocers. The group agreed and recommended that students study how the stores operated and what relationship they had to the community. They planned to research questions such as whether the owners did their banking in the neighborhood and their general views of residents in order to offer insights to the organization.

As I began to plan the project, it occurred to me that I knew nothing about the contexts into which I would be sending my students. On my way to CFSC meetings, I began visiting corner stores. CFSC members informed me that the majority of the owners were not from the neighborhood and were largely immigrants from the Middle East or South Asia. My observations seemed to confirm this. I learned what my students were soon to discover. I entered stores with the idea that I would buy something as a means to look inconspicuous, but the minute I entered I was peered at with a look that suggested that I was out of place. The owners or employees proceeded to appear preoccupied as if they were not going to be interested in engaging in discussion with anybody unless it involved business. On one occasion I was asked what I was selling and my first thought was that somehow my whiteness suggested to the owner that I was not there to buy. How would DePaul students—most of whom had limited research skills and a lack of knowledge of the neighborhood—break through social barriers constructed by the owners? Would they ever have the opportunity to conduct interviews?

My course was constructed with five clear objectives: first, gain a comprehensive understanding of how applied anthropology seeks to address local community-level problems; second, understand the ethical responsibility of anthropologists to protect research subjects; third, develop a sense of the variety of methodologies used by applied anthropologists; fourth, comprehend how applied anthropological research can directly or indirectly impact public policy; and fifth, articulate the various factors involved in the development of research projects with community-based organizations. These objectives were to be met through involvement in one of two projects on behalf of a community agency. The overall goal of the course and projects was to offer students a context for learning about the various goals, methods, and problems of anthropological practice.

Given that it was the first time the course was offered, I projected that enrollment would be low. The CFSC Corner Store project was designed to be small as was a second project designed to study the social organization of a neighborhood food pantry. In the weeks prior to the quarter, enrollment fluctuated around nine students and I speculated that four to five would work on each project. On the first day of class, only four students arrived. Shortly thereafter, another student dropped, leaving two students on the Corner Store Project and one on the Food Pantry Project.

Researching Corner Stores in Austin: Student Analysis of CBAR

Critical pedagogy is an approach to teaching that pushes students to confront dominant ways of thinking about, and behaving in, the world. The instructor generally guides students to question dominant ideologies in order to encourage them to think critically about knowledge and how it is produced. CBAR can further enhance the capacity of students to challenge existing social norms by moving them into physical and social spaces that may make them uncomfortable. I have learned that many students experience initial awkwardness as they enter fieldwork. These feelings typically emerge from their personal histories and changing sense of identity. Faculty have no control over the identities of students who enroll in their classes, yet the data resulting from CBAR projects always reflect a transformation in critical consciousness of individual students.

Like all researchers, students bring individual qualities that direct projects down particular pathways. Some will have difficulty breaking through social barriers to engage in a project while others will be comfortable in even the most unfamiliar settings. Ethnographic fieldwork as a research paradigm, in this regard, is particularly challenging for some students. It raises the bar by requiring that they become active participants while observing and getting to know others in ways that make their own presence seem mundane. This is not a problem for qualitative methods courses that assign students to conduct participant observation at the cafeteria, student union, or fitness center. It is certainly a challenge, however, when sending students off campus into places where they have little experience. For the two students who selected the Corner Store project, Austin was such a place. Neither had ever been to the neighborhood prior to the course, and one had never been to the West Side of Chicago.

In retrospect, there was a high probability that students in my course would have little knowledge of Austin. In 2003 the university reported its undergraduate enrollment as 60% white, 13% Latino, 10% African American, 9% Asian Pacific Islander, and 8% other (DePaul University, 2003a, p. 17). That same year, the university claimed to enroll a freshman class of 60% female and 40% male. Although the demographic makeup of a course can shift quite considerably from term to term, the three students remaining in the applied anthropology course (white females in their junior or senior year) reflected a trend in DePaul's overall enrollment. Furthermore, the students not only lived within the vicinity of the university, but none were originally from Chicago. In the few years they had lived in the city, however, they had learned the neighborhood boundaries.

Although the two students who researched corner stores shared certain demographic qualities, they were otherwise quite different. One was more comfortable with the idea of venturing into Austin and informally visiting stores, whereas the other saw this as extremely challenging. The latter claimed to be shy and said she felt awkward with the ethnographic practice of "hanging out." After my visits to the corner stores, I could see how this student might feel odd standing around in what were generally very small businesses where the owner was extremely attentive to the motives of patrons. For this reason I built into the project a process whereby the owners would be informed of the students' intentions prior to their visits. In the second week of class, I distributed to the students a list of more than 100 small grocers in Austin with contact information. Their assignment was to telephone as many as they could, explain their project, pose preliminary questions regarding the stores, and ask permission to visit the store to observe customers and interview the owner. For the student more comfortable with ethnographic research methods this task seemed tedious, unnecessary, and a waste of time. The other student found that the telephone conversations made her more comfortable about visiting and conversing with the store owners. In the end each student found her way into stores, but each took a different path to get there.

After we drove about the neighborhood during the first week of class, the student who was more comfortable with ethnographic research quickly began visiting stores and conversing with owners. Some were welcoming to her, and others more or less encouraged her to move on. The student who claimed to be more introverted telephoned stores until she found owners who were responsive, although she struggled to actually schedule visits and interviews. For weeks we conversed about her personal conflicts with the research and general fear of interviewing. Eventually, she did visit several stores, although she continued to have trouble attaining interviews from owners. Instead, she found a way to have informal conversations with owners and employees who permitted her to observe the stores. This resulted in a much richer account of how stores were organized than the other student's data, which came mostly from interviews. Each student found her individual niche in the project, a phenomenon I believe to be very common to CBAR.

Students submitted weekly field notes describing the interior and exterior of stores and conversations they had with owners. These included types of food, location of items on shelves, and how open owners were to conversing about their businesses and views of the surrounding community. The latter was a particular interest among CFSC members who were curious to find out whether corner stores would eventually be open to discussing or becoming part of an alternative food system involving the distribution of locally grown produce. In class we discussed the research findings and compared and contrasted food access in Austin with Lincoln Park. Questions emerged about why Austin residents had to go through so much trouble to gain access to healthy food options such as fresh fruits and vegetables. We discussed, for example, why a new chain supermarket opened across from a nearby public housing complex slated for demolition in a gentrifying neighborhood, while Austin—the largest neighborhood in Chicago—lacked such a store. These conversations invariably led students to note how race and class influenced where food resources were concentrated within the city. They began to see how public policies that encouraged gentrification were part of the same processes that led to the types of stores they observed in Austin and those they were familiar with in Lincoln Park.

At the end of the quarter, each student prepared a final report for CFSC. In summarizing their field notes and interviews, they were asked to illustrate their small but unique contribution to CFSC's broader research project. I provided guidelines for how to structure the reports, including descriptions of the research problem and questions defined by CFSC, as they understood them, their methodology, the neighborhood setting where they conducted research, case studies of particular stores, and finally their analysis of the data and recommendations. The students presented these reports at a CFSC meeting.

In the presentations each student outlined her project and highlighted some of the more unique discoveries from her field notes and interviews. For example, one student noted how a store precariously placed
bleach and laundry products adjacent to bags of flour and sugar and
above cereal without concern for possible contamination. Both students
also reported that they were surprised to find that several store owners
who lived outside the neighborhood patronized local banks, suggesting
they had some connection to the neighborhood. In general, however, the
students confirmed that the store owners were largely detached from the
community they served.

The most important finding presented by both students was the level
of importance store owners and employees placed on the surveillance of
customers. Ethnographic narratives offered insight into how the students'
own appearance as white females played a role in identifying the propen-
sity of store owners to respond coldly to and, as one student noted, keep
a "close watch" over store patrons. She wrote:

He noticed me as soon as I entered the store and came over to ask if
he could help me. I introduced myself and reminded him that we had
spoken over the phone some weeks ago. He then said that he had a feeling that I was from the university because I did not look familiar to him
or as though I was a "regular customer."

Students documented how owners and employers rarely spoke with
customers. This enhanced a general lack of trust that contributed to their
suspicion of all who entered the stores. In the end, as suggested by this
chapter's opening quotation, how the students sensed this lack of trust
was intimately tied to their identities and appearance. This lent them the
privilege of not being perceived as untrustworthy. An important part of
the students' recommendations presented to CFSC was to find ways to
build trust with the store owners.

Conclusions

Corner stores in neighborhoods like Austin are sites where contradictions
and failures of laissez-faire capitalism come alive. Large-scale food retail-
ers concentrate in gentrified neighborhoods and areas where they specu-

late a pending residential transition. Meanwhile, small-scale stores in neighborhoods like Austin seem to have little interest in the well-being of residents. In the absence of public policies that would encourage an economically just and equitable local food economy, residents in these neighborhoods resort to becoming suspects in stores largely owned by nonresidents. Alternatively, they have to find a way to shop outside their neighborhood, a common phenomenon in Austin. Such neighborhoods are what British social scientists have referred to as "food deserts" (Whelan, Wrigley, Warm, & Cannings, 2002). These are urban areas where residents depend on small stores with high prices and a paucity of fresh fruits and vegetables.

As a result of their research in the Austin food desert, anthropology students began to comprehend the role of race and class privilege in the structuring of food access. This illustrates an important sense in which CBAR can be a valuable pedagogical tool for unveiling unearned privilege. This is especially true for students who presume the economy is the product of "invisible hand" market forces that follow a fictitious law of supply and demand. The Corner Store Project illuminated for students the lack of local, state, and federal policy initiatives that could curb the seemingly unyielding social, political, and economic impact of the gentrification process. This is a process that has skewed urban food retailing toward only those places perceived by risk-averse corporations as having short-term profit potential. What the Corner Store Project also proved was that students can offer small contributions of knowledge to community efforts that create alternatives to the corporate food sector.

In a national survey DePaul students ranked themselves twice in five years as the happiest college students in the United States (Franek, 2003). At least part of the reason for their happiness is the aesthetic beauty of Lincoln Park and the material amenities that come with attending classes in a neighborhood redesigned to serve those with money. Cafes, restaurants, pubs, and taverns line the streets around the campus, and, as mentioned previously, the university itself provides an abundance of food choices. CBAR, as part of a broader DePaul University initiative to engage students in service-learning, pushes learning off campus into spaces where students are asked to research and problematize social inequities from a local perspective. The ensuing view from outside the bubble can encourage them to see their happiness in Lincoln Park in a critical light. As one of the Corner Store Project students noted in her final reflections, "This project has widened my view of the food system upon which we all to some extent depend and led to my further questioning of the system in place."

The use of CBAR in courses offers the potential for students to enhance their critical understanding of social issues. It is a pedagogy that explicitly compels them to look beyond their own privilege, to deconstruct their preconceptions, including those of low-income urban neighborhoods, and to identify qualities about themselves that they would not have recognized by attending traditional courses. Nonetheless, in cities like Chicago, where race and class divisions are ripe for social analysis, academicians must be mindful of history. CBAR almost always takes place in politically charged communities where research may be seen by some as a precursor to gentrification and thus simply another form of surveillance.

Endnotes

1) The quote is drawn from a final report submitted by a DePaul University undergraduate student to the Chicago Food Systems Collaborative in May 2003. The report was titled "Small Grocers and the Austin Community."

2) The core of the research was funded the W. K. Kellogg Foundation who had recognized the need to address food access in Austin.

3) I am especially thankful to LaDonna Redmond, Maureen Hellwig, Danny Block, Claire Kohrman, Joanne Kouba, Lara Jones, Bill Peterman, and Yolanda Suarez for allowing me to take part in the important work of CFSC.

References

Chicago Police Department Research and Development Division. (2004). *Chicago police department 2004 annual report.* Retrieved August 8, 2006, from: http://egov.cityofchicago.org/webportal /COCWebPortal/COC_EDITORIAL/04AR.pdf

Choksi, N. (2004, Winter). An Austin "snapshot:" A nine-week asset-based ethnography of a far West Side community. *Perspectives on Civic Activism and City Life, 3,* 1–13.

City of Chicago Department of Planning and Development. (2004). *City of Chicago community area map.* Retrieved October 2, 2006, from: http://egov.cityofchicago.org/city/webportal/home.do

Colias, M. (2005). *Neighbors divided over Chicago's crime-busting cameras.* Retrieved August 8, 2006, from: http://www.usatoday.com /tech/news/techpolicy/2004-04-30-chicago-police-cams_x.htm ?POE=TECISVA
DePaul University. (2003a). *2003 enrollment summary.* Chicago, IL: Author.

DePaul University. (2003b). *Mission statement.* Retrieved August 8, 2006, from the Steans Center for Community-based Service Learning web site: http://cbsl.depaul.edu//hm_mission.htm

Franek, R. (2003). *The best 351 colleges: 2004 Edition. The smart student's guide to colleges.* New York, NY: The Princeton Review.

Manley, T., Jr., Buffa, A. S., Dube, C., & Reed, L. (2006). Putting the learning in service learning: From soup kitchen models to the black metropolis model. *Education and Urban Society, 38*(2), 115–141.

Northern Illinois Planning Commission. (n.d.). *Profile of general demographic characteristics: 2000.* Retrieved October 2, 2006, from: http://www.nipc.org/test/DP_1234_CA_2000.xls

Pogge, J. (1992). Reinvestment in Chicago neighborhoods: A twenty - year struggle. In G. D. Squires (Ed.), *From redlining to reinvestment: Community responses to urban disinvestment* (pp. 133–148). Philadelphia, PA: Temple University Press.

Whelan, A., Wrigley, N., Warm, D., & Cannings, E. (2002). Life in a 'food desert.' *Urban Studies, 39*(11), 2083–2100.

Participatory Action Research and the University Classroom

2

Beth Skilken Catlett, Irene Clare Beck

The purpose of this chapter is to explore a feminist-informed participatory action research project in which DePaul University faculty, students in undergraduate classes, and community members have collaborated to address issues of social policy, advocacy, and community development. The project, "Teen Girls Re-Vision East Rogers Park," focused on life narrative interviews with a group of teen girls of color from low-income families. All girls were members of a thriving community-based leadership program in the East Rogers Park neighborhood of Chicago.

We aim to accomplish four ends. First, we explore the unique characteristics of a university environment that has facilitated the growth and development of progressive participatory action research. Second, we discuss those qualities that characterize our overall research agenda, with a particular focus on describing our course-based research model. This includes an examination of the ways in which this model differs from a traditional, hierarchical undergraduate classroom structure. Third, we introduce readers to our participatory action research project and offer an analysis of research planning and design. Here we also present a glimpse of our findings and demonstrate the processes through which we created mutually reinforcing synergies among research, teaching, and community engagement. Finally, we articulate a set of reflections on our work as a feminist-informed participatory action research collective.

Positive University Climate

In 2002 the authors of this chapter founded the Women and Gender Research Initiative at DePaul University. This initiative is housed within the Women's and Gender Studies Program. It is designed to promote community-based programs and research that inform the prevention of and intervention in gender-related oppressions. The initiative is committed to documenting, collecting, and making public the contributions of individuals whose lives reflect previously untold experiences and resilience. From 2003–2006 the initiative has developed, funded, and implemented four very successful community-based projects. Each of these projects (one of which is detailed later in this chapter) spurs the development of a curriculum that seeks to educate students in varied research processes. It also provides opportunities to participate in ongoing research projects and integrate those experiences with contextual course content. We strive to take students from content to methods and from academics to the real world of community engagement and grassroots organizing.

Our work has found substantial support at DePaul University, and we believe that DePaul offers a climate that is uniquely conducive to the development of such work. In particular, the vision and academic goals of the Women and Gender Research Initiative articulate well with DePaul's Vincentian purpose and mission. At the center of this mission is a commitment to involve the university deeply in the life of the surrounding urban communities by assisting them in finding solutions to their problems. Furthermore, the Vincentian approach involves a commitment to holistic and integrated educational processes in which we educate the heart as well as the head. The approach blends the humanistic and the professional, the abstract and the practical.

Beyond its Vincentian roots, three other institutions within the DePaul community have been especially valuable in terms of supporting and nurturing our commitment to participatory action projects. First is the Steans Center for Community-based Service Learning, which was founded to integrate the service concept into the university's curricula. At the center of the Steans Center's mission is a commitment to foster, through higher education, a deep respect for the dignity of all persons and to instill in students a dedication to service to others. Not only has the Steans Center supported our work financially, but it has also been instrumental in assisting and supporting the integration of service-learning pedagogy into our work.

Second, we have been fortunate to find a permanent home for many of our research materials in the special collections and archives section of the Richardson Library at DePaul University. The staff of special collections and archives has collaborated with us in many ways, contributing to the rich opportunities DePaul students and community members have had to engage with our participatory action research. These individuals have expanded their traditional services to make these research materials accessible in the present and in the future to all who are interested in learning from them.

Finally, the Women's and Gender Studies Program at DePaul University has been unwavering in their support of our work. Two leaders of the program have spanned the duration of our work, and both have had the vision that gave birth to and then nurtured our participatory action research collaborative. Our program structure and practices differ from more conventional academic institutional structures in a variety of ways, and we believe these differences to be quite positive. For instance, the very nature of the Women's and Gender Studies Program is interdisciplinary. Our faculty members are drawn from disciplines throughout the College of Liberal Arts and Sciences. Program faculty members' diverse areas of specialization are widely represented in their teaching, research, and community activism. Additionally, the program has welcomed adjunct faculty members to be full participants. In the case of our research initiative, the strong community ties of one of our founders— an adjunct faculty member—has been vital to the establishment and growth of our work. We were encouraged to explore ways in which our research interests might converge in undergraduate courses to broaden students' exposure to diverse populations and multiple oppressions. We also introduced students to the rigors and rewards of conducting feminist research. Indeed, our program has continually been open to the creation of new courses as well as the adaptation of existing ones. It is designed to integrate participatory action research as central to these curricula.

Overall Research Agenda

Our overall research agenda is to promote multidisciplinary collaborative study in the areas of gender, oppression, and resilience, providing opportunities for mutually reinforcing synergies between research, teaching, and community engagement. Our projects are aimed at working with community members to bring about social change through research that addresses social policy, advocacy, and community development. Toward these ends each research project is directed by a full-time faculty member who collaborates with student researchers to guide their partnership with members of community organizations and institutions. Additionally, we have created a course-based research model that develops curricula to educate students in varied research processes, provides opportunities to participate in ongoing research projects, and integrates those experiences with contextual course content.

Course-Based Research Model

By way of introduction, it is important to articulate the four central theoretical assumptions that underlie our course-based research model. First, our feminist theoretical grounding translates into a commitment to conducting research *for* and *with* our community participants, as opposed to conducting research *on* them (Cook & Fonow, 1990; Thompson, 1992). This feminist-informed research is intended to empower women and challenge inequalities of all kinds. It focuses on topics vital to the community members, gives voice to their experiences, and provides possible directions toward community change. By using our feminist framework, we hoped to ensure that research participants' priorities informed the project, rather than our own assumptions of what their priorities might or should be.

Second, we value an asset-based model that emphasizes research participants' strengths and resiliencies rather than the more pervasive deficit model. In the latter, culturally oppressed, marginalized individuals' experiences are often viewed as deficient in comparison to their more "privileged" counterparts. This does *not* mean that we fail to explore the complex challenges surrounding research participants' lives. Rather, we are committed to contextualizing these challenges and examining the social, economic, cultural, and historic forces that embed the participants' lives.

Third, to ensure that the action research projects are truly meaningful endeavors for the community organizations with which we collaborate, we have chosen to undertake only those projects that have been initiated by community organizations themselves. For instance, in both projects described later in this chapter, grassroots community organizations, with which one of us has had long-standing ties, approached us with requests for help. They each sought university collaboration and qualitative research that would give a wider audience and an enduring presence for the rarely heard voices of their constituents.

Finally, we are committed to an interactive model in which faculty, students, and community organizations participate from beginning to end of each research project. This means that we *all* collaborate fully in the various stages of research, including determining project design and scope, navigating emergent research focus, reviewing data that are collected and analyzed, shaping the written report, and staging public events at its completion.

With these theoretical assumptions as our basic scaffolding, we then design each participatory action research course so that we can provide ample flexibility to create a unique structure. Our goals are to educate students, expand their knowledge base, and challenge them to explore feminist research methodologies, while engaging with community organizations to meet vital research needs. For example, over the past few years, one of us has included a new focus on a participatory action research project in a lower division undergraduate course that is taught every year. The research project is offered as one of several research options from which students may choose. The other of us has framed an entire undergraduate seminar around an action research project. Students have chosen among varied assignments, all tied to the research. We have also created a new course for upper division undergraduate and graduate students to learn the qualitative research methodology of conducting life narrative research. Participating students are engaged in activist research with community-based organizations in direct application of these methodological approaches.

Beyond building in course flexibility, there are a variety of additional research issues that need to be negotiated as we implement this course-based research model. Time constraints and students' lack of prior research training are frequently cited professional concerns that can limit the substantive content of student-focused research (Fine, Torre, Boudin, Bowen, Clark, Hylton, et al., 2004). Indeed, DePaul's quarterly academic calendar yields 10-week courses, which, in practice, limits direct student involvement in research to approximately eight weeks. To address these concerns, two features have been included in all of our courses. First, each research project is ongoing, spanning several academic years. This requires that the research focus of a particular course in any given quarter be determined by the stage of the ongoing research process. While students learn about the purposes and methodologies of the entire project, their assignments are chosen from the work that remains to be done in the research. Second, all research materials are permanently archived in DePaul's Richardson Library. This includes individual student research papers, which are viewed as their contributions to the ongoing study, each representing one point of view at one point in time. In these ways, student assignments can transcend the limitations of a single course and a single individual's grasp of the subject matter by contributing to a larger body of research. Individual work may be valued for what it is: no more and no less than what each student is capable of producing. Moreover, the entire research process need not be compromised in any way by the inadequacies of an individual paper.

Assessment is, of course, an essential part of every course experience. However, it is particularly important in a course that engages students in participatory action research. As others have described, institutions committed to such nontraditional classroom endeavors must be able to demonstrate the impact of these initiatives to ensure quality for student and community participants, to justify resource investments, and to inform the improvement and expansion of such programs (Gelmon, Sherman, Gaudet, Mitchell, & Trotter, 2004). We align ourselves with those who hold that there are four primary reasons for assessments. The first is to improve student learning. The second is to provide immediate feedback so program leaders can make incremental changes and respond to identified needs and concerns. The third is to provide a basis for program planning and for redesign and substantive improvement. The fourth is to provide accountability for funding purposes. Additionally, researchers in community-university partnerships have established that such assessments can contribute to ensuring high-quality, enduring relationships among all participants, especially in light of the different concerns and expectations that faculty, students, and community partners may bring to a project. Beyond articulating what has been learned, assessment can also provide an opportunity to celebrate successes that have been achieved and can focus future planning to include new insights gained. Finally, it is vital that assessment outcomes be used to facilitate expansion of this methodology to other faculty, disciplines, and courses. By sharing lessons learned, assessment findings can identify significant factors for others who are considering similar work.

Perceived Strengths of Course-Based Research

In what some may consider an unconventional university classroom environment, as professors, we do not assume the role of chief content expert imparting all significant information. That is, we are not guided by the traditional assumption that the student is the only one who is to learn and the faculty member is the only teacher—one who lectures. Rather, as faculty members, we are the lead researchers and perhaps the primary facilitators of learning. We are engaged in a collaborative learning process in which everyone—faculty, students, and community members—is alternately learning from and teaching one another from their own experiences. The learning process is multifaceted, where students actively create their assignments, conduct research, and explore community needs. They also integrate this new knowledge with course readings, which traditionally have been the principal learning tools in universities.

Indeed, in our classrooms, students are expected to actively engage throughout the course in assignments as well as assessments, which are self- and faculty driven. This ongoing productive and reflective process stands in contrast to the traditional passive learner role that waits for an external evaluation from the teacher. Unlike most traditional course assignments, which may have little real-world relevance beyond earning course credit, students in research-based courses share in the reality of engaging in social justice-oriented research that has the potential of impacting public policy change. For the many students whom we find want to continue their research past the end of the course, there is the unique possibility for further collaboration with the faculty member, other academic colleagues, library archival research staff, and the community organization with which they have studied.

Perceived Challenges of Course-Based Research

Typical of most participatory action research courses, ours have demanded greater preparation time, even when repeatedly teaching a class. For instance, when a course begins, students may be unsure what to expect with this different course model and may take longer than in traditional courses to acclimate to their new learning environment. This process often requires greater faculty attention and interaction with individuals and student groups than in traditional classes. Guiding students toward a successful research experience includes helping them select a topic or focus that will be manageable for their research skills and experiential levels. Furthermore, there are substantially more ad hoc adjustments and modifications that are made throughout an individual course, based on class and research progress. Such adjustments are likely to include ongoing communications with the participating community organization. This typically requires a significant time commitment and negotiation of scheduling details.

An additional challenge that we have navigated in several of our courses involves the special ethical concerns that present themselves when undergraduate students are involved in research with vulnerable populations. We take seriously our commitment to conduct ethical research and our obligation to protect the rights and needs of our so-called subjects. We also take seriously our commitment to providing a full and robust educational experience for our undergraduate students. On occasion, these two commitments may be in tension, because relatively inexperienced and unprepared undergraduate researchers involve themselves in community-based projects. We are mindful of the challenge this tension presents and continuously strive to be creative and resourceful in maximizing our ability to deliver on our dual commitments.

Participatory Action Research Exemplar: Teen Girls Re-Vision East Rogers Park

When we began this research project, we hoped it would enhance the empowerment of a group of urban teen girls of color from low-income families who were members of a teen leadership program at Family Matters, a community organization in the East Rogers Park neighborhood of Chicago. A brightly colored banner welcomes all who enter the teen girls' room at Family Matters: "We see the truth . . . then we speak our minds." This message was just the reason we were there.

The teen girls from Family Matters were originally prompted to forge their collaboration with us after they completed a community action project that led to some unintended negative consequences. When the teens looked for community background information for this action project, they were stunned by the absence of any public collection of photographs or written history about people of color in East Rogers Park. Additionally, they were offended by the descriptions of their neighborhood that were posted on various web sites. They were appalled by and resisted perspectives that characterized their local streets as full of danger emanating from crime, drugs, prostitution, or from poor immigrants and people of color. Those negative images demeaned streets they saw as far from mean. They saw those views as incomplete stereotypes excluding diverse individuals whom they knew as neighbors, relatives, friends, role models, and mentors. They also strongly felt that such negative stereotypes most certainly did not apply to them. So a project that had started as a learning tool for youth leadership ultimately left these youth feeling disempowered, invisible, and voiceless.

The director of the teen girls' program approached one of us, with whom she has had long-standing professional ties, and asked if there was a way to help the teens express their own perspectives. She said she hoped that by collaborating with us and our university students, the girls might continue their powerful learning and sharing with others. Thus, as faculty members in the Women's and Gender Studies Program at DePaul University, we came to plan with these young women ways to give voice to their experiences and views. They lived in a gentrifying neighborhood and were facing a host of age-, family-, and community-related issues. We also sought ways to connect the teens with our DePaul University students in two of our undergraduate courses. They designed a life narrative project in which the teens would be interviewed and their words developed into a published text, giving voice to their own stories to be shared with the community. We hoped that through this process, our students would increase their awareness of a central objective of feminist participatory action research: that the complexity of diversity issues and interlocking oppressions of sexism, racism, and classism can profoundly impact the lives of real young women in their own urban community.

We chose the telling of the teens' stories as the form of our research, a methodology that is grounded in the feminist belief that life narratives are central to the existence of social life (Thompson, 2000). The details of their narratives may be contradictory, Thompson maintains, but that does not make them right or wrong. The teens' views and experiences are not put forth as being representative of a universal social life. Yet these narratives have real value to the tellers and their listeners. The narrative process involved the active participation of the teens as they constructed ways of describing and accounting for themselves to their listeners and readers.

Life narratives have a significant place in feminist research. As social science researcher Annette Kuhn (1985) argues, telling stories is central to constructing self-identity, although the memories included in such stories are personal, the connections they make transcend the individual teller. These stories create a record of the lives of marginalized women, capturing their ways of knowing and seeing the world.

Grounded in our feminist research approach, we have been committed to conducting research for and with these teen girls, as opposed to conducting research on them (Cook & Fonow, 1990; Thompson, 1992). This project focused on topics vital to the teens' lives, giving voice to their experiences and providing possible directions toward community change. At the same time, we have been keenly aware of the importance of the relationship between ourselves and our young participants. Rather than exploit their stories based on power inherent in the position of university researchers, we sought to strike a balance among us. We recognized that the teens' voices must be clearly communicated on the written page. We hoped this would ensure that the teens' priorities stood out, rather than the priorities that we might have presumed were, or should be, those of adolescent females. Additionally, it was critical that the teens realized they were perceived by others as collaborators—rather than objects—in this research process.

As we have faced these challenges, we have also benefited from prior exploration of these issues by other feminist researchers. They, too, have struggled to find ways to interpret the voices of their interviewees. In such studies, it is the researcher who ultimately must provide some framework for understanding the views and stories of the participants. Final responsibility for analyzing their stories must also remain with the researcher. Three guidelines emerged from our exploration of the literature: first, engage in ongoing collaboration with the interviewees as their stories and views are analyzed (Gluck & Patai, 1991); second, continually reflect on our own position as it affects our understanding and research process (Franz & Stewart, 1994); and third, realize that no one source of knowledge provides a complete picture (Sollie & Leslie, 1994).

We met with the teen girls several times before our university courses began, planning with them the design of the research project and the focus of the interview questions. As an introduction for our students, we embedded background information about the teen girls' program in an extended contextual essay about the project and a brief history of this often transitioning neighborhood.

Early in our courses, we explored the topic of privilege and many ways that it presents in society as well as within our own classrooms. We examined prevalent biases and stereotypes about teen girls, their experiences, families, schools, and neighborhoods. Then we explored our own expectations, attitudes, fears, and hopes about engaging these teen girls and this project. In small group exercises, we analyzed our multiple identities and myriad ways in which we all differ from *others*. We then read and discussed ways to overcome some barriers separating individuals and cultural, economic, and racial/ethnic groups. We also considered methods of building bridges across those divides, seeking commonalities, and the merits of attempting such an undertaking. As the final step in this initiation phase of our courses, each student was given an assignment to write a three- to five-page paper titled "Who Am I?" The papers were to be written as a hypothetical introduction to the group of teen girls in our research project, indicating ways in which our students might self-identify their place or position in terms of race, class, gender, and sexual orientation. They also examined their traits, characteristics, preferences, and experiences that could accurately portray themselves as unique individuals. We hope that writing a paper such as this one provided students with the opportunity to consider the biases and assumptions that they may bring to our research project.

Our students eagerly engaged in the project and provided invaluable insights. For example, as they worked in small groups to critique our interview protocol, they soon identified a bridge to the teen girls. They were only a few years older than the teen participants, ranging in age from 18 to 22 years old, and this likeness helped us as we considered vital issues of creating rapport. Indeed, their suggestions about approachable words and phrases allowed us to relate more easily to the teens. In addition they read transcript excerpts and articulated emerging themes. In readings and discussions, they explored particular risks that the teens might be exposed to. At the same time, however, they became critical analysts in rejecting generalized assumptions about the "victim" image that many readings confer when portraying low-income urban girls of color. Our students became advocates for these teens, wanting the best for them and wishing they could continue with us on the project as the courses ended.

As the school year wound down, we all began to think about the next stages of the project. We hired two of the teen girls as interns over the summer to serve as research advisors on the project. They planned with us the publication of the research report and public events at the completion of the project the following spring. Each week they read text excerpts and advised on whether the teens' voices were coming through accurately. They met with the university publications staff to choose layout, color, and text designs and learned simple ways to convert narratives into dramatic presentations from another faculty member who specializes in dramaturgy. They attended a social justice legacy exhibit celebrating the lives of a group of Chicago women leaders. They took rolls of photos, collected poetry written by their peers, and wrote some of their own. They toured DePaul's Richardson Library archives and saw where their materials would be permanently stored (near artifacts related to Napoleon and Charles Dickens). The following year, the teen girls and their families and friends joined the DePaul faculty and students and members of their neighborhood and the DePaul communities at a press conference on the research report. The teens also presented a dramatic performance to celebrate the publication.

From the inception of this project, we were committed to creating visibility for these teen girls' insights and perspectives. The publication of our research monograph and the live dramatic performance were designed to communicate our main research findings to a broader public. A glimpse of these findings indicates that several themes were particularly prominent in these girls' lives. First, we saw paradoxical perspectives emerge as the teens talked about their community. Their narratives were often layered with ambivalence, complexities, and contradictions. The teens recognized the dangers in their neighborhood, yet they also voiced a strong sense of pride as well the opinion, "this is *my* community."

A second prominent theme involved street safety. Specifically, we saw that the teen girls viewed sexual harassment, both verbal and physical, on the street as normal everyday interactions, although they said they were frustrating, annoying, and sometimes frightening. The teen girls also decried what they saw as a lack of serious attention paid by the police to these matters. All of these incidents have been repeated frequently in public, in clear sight, and within earshot of other adults who do not stop these behaviors. As a result, the teens have come to view these offenses as virtually unstoppable.

Third, the teen girls' interviews showed a deep concern about the gentrification of East Rogers Park. Many of the teens' families, friends, and neighbors have been displaced while they search—often unsuccessfully—to find a new way to stay in their rapidly changing neighborhood. Furthermore, the teens were very troubled that many low-income families seemed forced to confront these unsought challenges in isolation.

When talking about school and friends, we saw that these teen girls are smart, committed, and hard working. We also saw that there is a real risk of their losing that focus in the absence of institutional supports. Their primary concerns revolved around peer-related issues. For instance, classroom behavioral disruptions, bullying, and peer violence were primary concerns. Moreover, friendships—with other girls and with boys— were often complex and troubling to many of the teen girls.

Finally, and of particular note, we concluded that our work with these teens dispels the view—perpetuated in our culture and in social science research—of the pathological single-parent family headed by a woman. These girls' descriptions of their families broke the stereotypes. Although the families were by no means perfect, the girls' descriptions were characterized by love, support, and commitment. Moreover, we were impressed with the active presence of positive male figures even in the absence of live-in biological fathers. We saw and heard many examples of the general need of every family to have multiple external supports.

Reflections, Conclusions, and Future Considerations

After reflecting on the last several years of integrating feminist-informed participatory action research projects into our courses, several insights have emerged that are particularly valuable in terms of considering future research and course development. As an initial matter, we recognize that a scholarly focus on participatory action and community-based work is still not considered mainstream at many universities in terms of professional evaluations and assessments. Moreover, and of particular importance, we also recognize that the type of collegial collaborations that we have forged are not always encouraged in traditional academic structures. That being said, we have found our fully developed professional collaborations enormously productive and enriching. For instance, our collaboration with the special collections and archives section of the Richardson Library at DePaul University has created rich opportunities for students and faculty members. The library staff has a unique knowledge base and innovative research skills that help to make research materials accessible and useful. Additionally, it is rare for two faculty members to have the opportunity to work so closely together on joint projects over such an extended time period. Our experience has convinced us that this type of partnership greatly enhances our work and lives.

The project discussed in this chapter has prompted continued reflection about how to best accommodate the different levels of preparation that students bring to our classrooms. We are mindful of the need to effectively assess students' skill levels in qualitative research and also to work diligently to help students shape specific research tasks. In addition we are committed to meeting the challenge of ensuring a successful educational experience for students and of developing a research project that upholds high quality and rigorous scientific standards.

Our commitment to the community-based model translates into action research projects in which organizational investment and "ownership" are critical. Indeed, most of the projects we have chosen to undertake are those that have been initiated by the community organizations themselves. The project discussed in this chapter resulted from an organization that sought collaboration with our university to give a wider voice to their organizational constituency. As we reflect on future projects, we recognize that our commitment to a community-based action research model may take on several different forms and that the initiation process will likely vary.

For example, one of our current projects falls squarely within such a community-initiated model. The Illinois Coalition Against Domestic Violence (ICADV)—one of the oldest and largest statewide coalitions dedicated to eliminating domestic violence—contacted us to seek out an Illinois academic institution to help them conduct an oral history of their organization. The two of us share professional backgrounds that specialize in analyzing domestic violence issues, conducting oral history research, and writing about women activists. We therefore agreed that this project sounded intriguing and began work. Students, faculty, and ICADV members are currently working together to create oral history interviews with founding members. They are also researching the collection of files that document the history of this organization within the broader context of the statewide and national struggle against domestic violence during the decades of ICADV's existence (1978–present). These historical records, along with transcripts and tapes of the oral history interviews, will be permanently archived in DePaul University's Richardson Library Special Collections and Archives.

Another project, developed somewhat differently, focuses on prevention of relationship violence among teens and grew out of our collaboration with domestic violence activists in the Chicago community. Working with community activists, we needed to generate interest on the part of the Chicago Public Schools, discussing with them how a partnership with DePaul University would be beneficial to the students and families in their communities. We collaborated with faculty and administrators from a variety of Chicago Public High Schools and discussed the benefits of a program that included service, learning, and research components in which DePaul University would partner with schools to create opportunities for teens. The goals are to increase teens' awareness and understanding of the types of relationship violence and to practice and observe actual relationship dynamics and interactions. The program aims to expand their exposure to sources of assistance in school and the community and to enhance their own empowerment by advocating for healthy, safe relationships and by forming a community action project.

As we reflect upon the work we have done, we recognize the various ways in which we carve out distinct participatory action research projects, as well as the specific forms they take in our university classrooms. We are also mindful that our work clearly builds upon the work of numerous others yet simultaneously strikes out in unique ways. And as is perhaps best reflected in the distinct manner in which each project got underway, each individual project presents unique opportunities and challenges that we are committed to negotiating within our feminist-informed research collective.

References

Cook, J. A., & Fonow, M. M. (1990). Knowledge and women's interests: Issues of epistemology and methodology in feminist sociological research. In J. M. Nielsen (Ed.), *Feminist research methods: Exemplary readings in the social sciences* (pp. 69–93). Boulder, CO: Westview Press.

Fine, M., Torre, M. E., Boudin, K., Bowen, I., Clark, J., Hylton, D., et al. (2004). Participatory action research: From within and beyond prison bars. In L. Weis & M. Fine (Eds.), *Working method: Research and social justice* (pp. 95–120). New York, NY: Routledge.

Franz, C. E., & Stewart, A. J. (Eds.). (1994). *Women creating lives: Identities, resilience, and resistance.* Boulder, CO: Westview Press.

Gelmon, S., Sherman, A., Gaudet, M., Mitchell, C., & Trotter, K. (2004). Institutionalizing service-learning across the university: International comparisons. In M. Welch & S. H. Billig (Eds.), *New perspectives in service-learning: Research to advance the field* (pp. 195–219). Greenwich, CT: Information Age Publishing.

Gluck, S. B., & Patai, D. (Eds.). (1991). *Women's words: The feminist practice of oral history.* New York, NY: Routledge.

Kuhn, A. (1985). *Power of the image: Essays on representation and sexuality.* New York, NY: Routledge.

Sollie, D. L., & Leslie, L. A. (1994). *Gender, families, and close relationships: Feminist research journeys.* Thousand Oaks, CA: Sage.

Thompson, J. (2000). *Women, class and education.* New York, NY: Routledge.

Thompson, L. (1992). Feminist methodology for family studies. *Journal of Marriage and the Family, 54*(1), 3–18.

Healthy Wednesdays in Our Hood: An Exploration of an Anthropological Service-Learning With Premeds[1]

Sam Beck

During the spring 2005 semester I discussed the Skills Academy with Father Jim. He first organized it in 1997 as an after-school recreation program in Bedford-Stuyvesant, Brooklyn. At the time Jim worked out of Mt. Sinai Roman Catholic Church (not the actual name), a parish started by Puerto Ricans in the 1950s when they migrated to New York City in large numbers. Jim is an Irish priest who grew up on Long Island and speaks fluent Spanish. Today, the number of Puerto Ricans in the area is in sharp decline and the parish is made up of a mixture of people. Jim started the Skills Academy, a boys' program, not so much as a service for parishioners, but as a service to the community at large. He developed an after-school recreation program into a program that supports middle school and early high school students' successful social, ethical, and professional engagement in society, with particular emphasis on college preparation.

To provide a thumbnail demographic picture of Bedford-Stuyvesant (Bed-Stuy), I list information provided by the Citizens' Committee for Children of New York City (2005). Of the 145,269 Bed-Stuy residents in 2003, 76% were African American and 18.3% Latino. About one-third of the population was under 18 years old. African-American children under 18 years old made up 77.8% and Latinos 20.7 %. Household income ranged from below $15,000 or 36.8%, to $75,000 or 12.6%

(Citizens' Committee for Children of New York City, pp. 196–208). These figures demonstrate that Bed-Stuy is one of the poorest areas of New York City and primarily black—people of African heritage predominate here, even when identifying as Latino; the impact of this type of urban poverty is particularly dramatic on children and youth of color (particularly children under 18 years old).

In the spring 2005 term the Cornell University Urban Semester Program (CUSP) contributed two undergraduate students to work with the students in the Skills Academy. CUSP students worked in small groups, providing individual casework and academic enrichment opportunities, including exposing the youths to the professional world and assisting in recreation activities to foster positive development. CUSP students and the Skills Academy students benefited from their participation in the design of an academic enrichment program. We intentionally put the two groups together to enable them to cross social, cultural, economic, and racial boundaries, which they would not otherwise cross.

With this in mind and the spring 2005 semester experience behind us, Jim and I decided to continue our relationship in the summer, at which time I had 11 premed students in an eight-week, three-credit, experience-based learning program for which we developed a community service-learning project. Central to what we were planning was for the two sets of young people (13–15 years and 18–23 years) to get to know each other. In other words, they were to cross ethno-cultural, socioeconomic, and racial boundaries. The Cornell University students and the teens would go into the neighborhood to take photographs of "healthy places" (Wang & Burris, 1994; Wang, Wu, Zhan, & Carovano, 1998).

Community service-learning is a way of learning and teaching. The approach focuses on service projects that enhance classroom course work. A more critical approach focuses on service as the principal device for learning. The goal of community service-learning is to increase student awareness of civic responsibilities while providing support for a community in need. Pedagogically, service-learning provides students with the context and conditions for critical thinking through reflection.

The CUSP students spent four days each week at the New York Presbyterian Hospital in rotations of their own choosing. On Wednesdays they met with me for reflection seminars. They also met with medical practitioners from the hospital to discuss the various aspects of medical culture and practice. In addition, we met with a variety of local-level, community-based religious practitioners who spoke to us about their cultural traditions in relation to healing practices. In the afternoons, from 4:00 p.m. to 5:30 p.m., we assembled in the Mt. Sinai Church basement to meet with the Skills Academy students.

The Wednesdays were designed around an academic experience-based learning pedagogy that used reflexivity and reflective practices as mechanisms for self-directed learning.[2] The students learned skills central to medical practice, including building relationships and communicating effectively across cultural differences. These meetings were also designed to complement and support an aspect of premed learning generally not given much weight in medical schools except through volunteer projects: the giving of oneself without looking for rewards. We felt this experience to be especially important for the students involved in the project.

The students who entered CUSP, a 15-credit Cornell University academic semester in New York City, most frequently self-identified as coming from homogeneous communities. They generally referred to their white, relatively affluent suburbs. The exceptions were a small number of students of color from low-income households and communities. They found their way to Cornell University's undergraduate programs as a result of parochial school attendance and strong, education-oriented households in which they were socialized. Ironically, students from both groups found the campus to be the most diverse place in which they had lived.

The absence of physical and spatial contact between affluent and impoverished communities in their settlements is a product of an apartheid-like system of segregation that is not perceived as a healthy outcome among those who desire to see a more equitable American society (Kozol, 2005). One core value accepted by the middle class, and propagated by U.S. policies, is that educational advancement is the road to success and healthy lifestyles. The eight-week CUSP program incorporated reasonably achievable goals and created conditions to release negative stereotypes while expanding opportunities for higher education.

Father Jim knew the Skills Academy students in his program through the contacts he had made on the street. He would spend time in front of his church and talk to the students and their family members as they walked or biked by. Almost all of the students whom we got to know through the program were black Latinos. Many lived to play basketball. When we asked them what they wanted to do when they grew up, inevitably they responded, "play basketball for the NBA." Even if they realized this was an unrealistic fantasy, their passion for basketball was high, and they would play whenever possible. In thinking about what we would do with them, we did not take this fully into account.

The work that Jim was carrying out with Bed-Stuy students during the academic year was based on a contractual arrangement through which they had to attend the Skills Academy program regularly. Otherwise they would not be able to play basketball during the summer if no such contract were in place. Nor did we (or they) have access to a basketball court. This meant that we were completely dependent on the Skills Academy students to show up, because they wanted to be there for their own sake or out of loyalty to Jim and his staff.

The Project

I felt that one of the most effective approaches to learning across identity boundaries and from each other is to engage in "project learning," so I decided to use photographs as a means for capturing the imagination of youngsters. This approach had worked well in the 1990s when I assembled South Bronx youths and Cornell University undergraduate students for projects in the South Bronx neighborhood. By having the students work on projects together in small groups, they would talk to each other about their lives and ask questions that they might have been too intimidated to ask in more formal classroom settings. The project became the driving force behind the learning that took place. This learning was achieved without students and other participants actually being aware that teaching and learning were occurring.

In the first session, the students and I discussed appropriate topics for involving youths. I wanted to distance us from the typical approach in such projects. According to Joe Hall, the executive director of the Ghetto Film School in the Bronx, disadvantaged youths are asked to take photographs of their neighborhood, and inevitably they are led to photograph the least attractive parts. This only enforces the stereotypical images of the urban poor and their low-income environments. I was not interested in the Skills Academy students reproducing hegemonized images of their neighborhood (Fanon, 1963; Gramsci, 1957; Klein, 1974). That is to say, I did not want them to confirm some of my students' assumptions about low-income, poorly supported communities of color. That is what they would have done had we given them the cameras to take photographs of their neighborhood. In my separate conversations with low-income youths in their neighborhoods, they usually discussed the negative aspects of their lives. While there is nothing wrong with this, I did not want my students exposed to this kind of attitude. Instead, I hoped to expose them to the idea of an asset-based approach. We wanted the youths to focus on the glass as half full. Joe Hall,[3] also a community-building expert in the South Bronx, refers to this approach as "youth at risk of success," inverting the pejorative understanding our society has of young people who learn to survive in low-income neighborhoods. By using this method I hoped that the youths and CUSP students would recognize existing strengths that could in turn build their confidence and enhance their skills to excel at new challenges. Jim led us to believe that the Bed-Stuy youths could use some academic support and develop some alternative visions for their future. We could help them create a vision of college and aim higher to achieve careers in professions that Cornell students usually strive for. Jim wanted the youngsters to broaden their views of what was possible by inspiring a more expansive future vision.

While thinking about this, I was caught in a paradox. Our ideas about the lives of the youths were based on assumptions that they should aspire to professional work and consider that as success. This would be their new vision of their future. That certainly is what my students believed and valued. We never questioned this issue as we implemented the project with the youths by giving them disposable cameras with which to shoot pictures. I now wonder how hard we should have pressed this agenda of cultural change. We wanted them to change their value system to one that was shaped by the privileged white middle classes. What if their values and understanding of success were not oriented toward socioeconomic mobility? Mobility here is not only one of class and economic position but of geography as well. Upward mobility usually means moving out of the "ghetto."

According to the introduction of the published brochure documenting our work, my students wrote:

> We focused our efforts on demonstrating ways of reflection on the health and well-being of the community. Each of us paired up with a motivated young man and asked him to show us places in the neighborhood that he thought were crucial to his health, both mental and physical. We guided the boys in photographing such places, all the while socializing and exchanging experiences amongst ourselves. Beyond socializing and recreation, we sat down with the students one-on-one and encouraged them to constructively write about the pictures they had taken and the role those places played in their lives. (CUSP Students, 2005)

Having the relationship with Father Jim enabled us rapidly to build rapport with the Skills Academy students, whom Jim knew well. He knows their names, their families, where they live, and whom they hang out with. He knows their daily schedules.

Our Wednesday afternoon visits to the Bed-Stuy church was often punctuated by rain. The torrential downpours frustrated us just about every week of our project. What made it particularly maddening was that, because of the rain, we were never sure who would show up to our sessions. Even when it was not raining, we were uncertain *when* the youths would arrive. Sometimes we had to track them down at the local basketball court. We would also call their homes to make sure that they would attend. We had several youths on whom we could depend, especially three brothers whose parents made sure they were present and then returned home promptly. But 10 or so other youths moved in and out over the course of seven weeks. At the time, I did not feel that the group participated consistently enough for the CUSP students to experience solidarity with the youths. They also did not learn enough from them to change their stereotyped beliefs of the inner-city youth. However, it turned out to be "my problem"— prejudging my students, rather than keeping an open mind as I did with the Bed-Stuy youths.

What was striking about the summer was that the asset-based approach took hold of the CUSP students in a way that I did not predict. Was it because they were already service oriented? Or was it because they hoped to become doctors and somehow were predisposed to position themselves as helpers or compassionate and empathetic individuals? As premeds, carrying out clinical, primarily shadowing experiences in New York Presbyterian Hospital, they had already been exposed to people who had to negotiate the most vulnerable circumstances of their lives. Did this have an impact on them when working with the youths? Were they able to transfer this kind of knowledge to a different group of people experiencing a different sort of vulnerability? What was clear to me while watching them interact with the youths was their sincere effort to communicate with them through the project and their commitment to completing the project.

During our first session, we did icebreakers and tried to tell personal stories. We all sat on metal folding chairs in the hot basement room under the church. The CUSP students tried very hard to engage the Skills Academy students who chatted among themselves, an activity they enjoyed each time we met with them. The second week we paired the youths with the CUSP students to take photographs of the neighborhood. We learned from our interactions with them that it was better to create smaller groups. This is because, as Jim told me as an aside, "they are intimidated," an explanation of what I had perceived as their shyness. In the following three weeks, the CUSP students and the youths sat down with the photographs to write captions. The cast of young people changed every week, with some not returning and new ones joining our group.

The CUSP students adjusted rapidly to the changing cast of youth, explaining the project to newcomers. From time to time, we had to deal with unacceptable behavior. For example, one of the newcomers brought his cell phone on which he had recorded music that he insisted on playing at the loudest volume. When politely asked, he turned down the volume or just turned it off. When the youths lost interest in a given task, the CUSP students motivated them to stay on target.

By the third week, the Skills Academy students had chosen the photographs for which they would develop captions. By this time we recognized that we would have to explain what we were doing with the project each time because of newcomers who were joining our activities. We told them that the photographs and captions would be used to produce a publication and we would have two poster presentations in our space in the basement with invited guests and another one at the Cornell Weill Medical College Department of Public Health. For the youths who were with us at all of our meetings, the idea of traveling to Manhattan was exciting. Jim considered this to be particularly important. It is common for these young people from low-income neighborhoods to be virtually confined in their own neighborhoods. They develop a powerful sense of belonging and strong bonds with family members and kin living close by. Their relationships with long-lasting friends and peers also are important to them.

My students were particularly concerned about the youths taking pictures of people, believing this to be unethical. They wanted to protect people from the intrusion of cameras and imposed this rule on the youths who followed their instructions and for the most part only took photographs of the built environment. The captions they wrote for the pictures revealed their identification and their activities there. This demonstrated to us how important the neighborhood was to them and the meaning they associated with particular places. The examples below illustrate this point.

Luis, who sported a yellow basketball jersey and a white do rag, wrote the following caption for a photograph of a school building:

> This is where I went to school from kindergarten to third grade. I have a lot of memories there. I met my first best friend there. That's where I first started learning. I liked my gym teacher because he taught us a lot of games. We learned how to play "Steal the Bacon," which is a basketball game. I liked another teacher, Miss Singleton. She taught me how to multiply. My favorite subjects are math and language arts. I liked my principal because he got me out of a lot of trouble like fights. My little broth-

er just graduated kindergarten of the same school, so it is
a place that means a lot to my family.

Billy, 12 years old, is small for his age but held his own with the
slightly older boys. He wrote the following caption for a photograph of a
corner playground:

> I picked this picture because this is the park I grew up in.
> It gives me memories: good ones, happy ones, and
> healthy ones. This is the park where I used to swing real-
> ly high on the swings, and where I shot my first basket-
> ball. This park makes me feel healthy and makes me feel
> like I'm home. If new people came to the community I
> can show them around and make friends with them.

Kaliek, who is 15 years old and showed up sporadically, wrote:

> This is a picture of a sneaker store. I buy my shoes here
> sometimes and I get my haircut next door. When you go
> to this sneaker store, you have to save more money to
> buy shoes than in regular sneaker stores. I go there with
> my friends and my girlfriend used to live around there.
> My school is also down the block from there and a lot of
> my friends live around there too. They have my favorites,
> Nike, Jordan, and Timberland's. I have about five pairs
> of sneakers now. On the same street there's a candy store
> that I go to after I get my hair cut. Also, when I am
> around this block, I go to the DVD store. There's a game
> store too. I like to go to buy some adventure and sports
> video games.

Lionel, 13 years old, came each and every Wednesday. He was generally quiet and reserved compared to the other more boisterous boys. He
has ambitions of becoming a lawyer. He thoughtfully wrote the caption
for a photograph of a fenced-in vegetable garden:

I like this picture because it shows me that people in the city care about plants. Plants are important because they provide food and they also give us oxygen in order to live. This makes plants healthy. I also like that this picture shows green life in this polluted city. This shows that people take the time to help the plants grow, which means that the people must also be healthy because they can physically care for them. I think we should have more plants around in our environment to show that we also care about our city.

For a photograph of a school entranceway with four doors, one of which was open, swinging out, Harry (13 years old) wrote:

I think about school as somewhere you can learn new things. I think it is a step closer to your future. If I go to school I can try to succeed at my goal of being a basketball player. When I think of school it brings back memories of when I was a little kid. I hope I can succeed at my goal by going to school. The skills I learned in 2nd grade were math and reading. They helped me because without math or reading I wouldn't be where I am right now. Math and reading are in mostly every subject. Without math, you can't count your money and without reading you can't read stories or important signs. I have learned that math and reading are very important and healthy skills.

Marvin wrote the caption for a photograph of a basketball hoop without a net and a backboard:

This basketball hoop is on my favorite court. I love to play here because it is the biggest court and it is the closest one to home. I've been playing here for eight years and it helps me keep in shape. I love the excitement of playing basketball.

Leron wrote the caption for a photograph of a McDonald's Restaurant taken from under an elevated train:

> I go to McDonald's with my friends and we talk. I get a #3 and a vanilla milkshake. We go after school when we are done playing basketball. When I go to McDonald's I see the same people that I know and I feel safe. When we are done we all go to one person's house and play video games. Then I go home. At home, I help straighten up the living room and I have dinner. My favorite dinner is fried chicken. I am thankful for my big family and big group of friends. Also, I am thankful for my twin brother. He is really smart. We get along really well. He is my best friend.

Harry wrote the caption for a photograph of an entrance to a school:

> I like school because I can talk to all of my friends. I like school because I can go outside play basketball and football with my friends. I like school because it's important to learn and it will help me do great things. I like school because of the teachers.

Martell wrote the caption for a photograph of a hospital building:

> I feel safe with a hospital in my neighborhood because when somebody gets hurt or sick, they can go there. A very few weeks ago, I had a big cut and I had to go to the hospital. It happened when I was playing outside and I hit my leg on a big piece of glass. With the hospital there, I felt safe. If it hadn't been there, I would have lost a lot of blood.

For a photograph of the youths playing basketball on a playground in the middle of a neighborhood block, David wrote:

Basketball is healthy for me because after I have a good meal I can go play basketball to digest the food that I just ate. I play to get better and take basketball to the farthest level I can. I use it to take out my energy frustration. Basketball is fun because you can play with your friends and also meet new people. I play basketball as much as I can. One day I hope I can build a good career and relationships with other people playing basketball.

For a photograph of some of the CUSP students with the youths eating pizza Martell wrote:

This picture is everybody having fun and eating pizza. People from college are helping kids and teaching them about college. I like that because it gives me ideas about the future. When I grow up I want to be a basketball player. It makes me happy to play basketball and to have friends. I like to box also because I like to knock people out. It feels good boxing and having friends and playing basketball.

Based on this experience we can say that both CUSP students and the Skills Academy students succeeded in demonstrating the power of asset-based learning and thinking. One of my students, Jenn (19 years old and from a white midwestern family) remarked:

Working with the kids from Bed-Stuy has been a pleasure. I am so impressed by the way they have responded to our program. They were so eager to take pictures and have been really excited about showing us their community and things that make them proud about it.

Ivan, an immigrant from Russia, was the only rising sophomore in the group; everyone else was a junior or senior. He wrote, "Healthy Wednesdays was an amazing way to spend one afternoon a week with a unique group of youngsters." This project benefited both the young men who participated and the Cornell students. Although we set out to reflect on aspects of community health and expose the young men to the vigor of college life, we soon found ourselves exploring the depths of a lifestyle novel to our own understanding and forging relationships much more meaningful than we could have imagined. With their forceful dedication to succeed where others had failed and their perseverance, these vibrant individuals opened up my eyes to the endless possibilities that lay before me. I want to thank them for broadening my horizons.

Writing about one of the youths with whom she worked, Katie remarked:

> He went on to write about what an opportunity this program is for both sides. He really has a renewed respect for the future and what it holds for him. He said that having us there is a good influence on him and his friends.

Shiva, a student of Indo-Jamaican descent, was older than the others at 24 years. She commented:

> I could see myself in some of these kids. Being faced with an upward road, where nothing is handed to you and nothing is certain. I absolutely enjoyed working with these kids but feel like the time spent was so short. I got to know Marvin a little and I'm convinced that he can accomplish anything he puts his mind to. He has this quiet confidence that makes him see obstacles as challenges and I wish him the best in all he tries.

David, an 18 year old Chinese American, wrote:

> To say that this project exposed me to people and places that I would never have had the opportunity to interact with, is quite the understatement. [T]his public health oriented project with these young adolescent males in the Bedford-Stuyvesant neighborhood of Brooklyn introduced me to a group of kids and a part of New York

City that was so incredibly different than what I was used to. Working with these young people in this neighborhood has taught me so much that a book, a lecture, a professor, and even a hospital never could.

I learned from Billy and the rest of the Bed-Stuy students how adolescents behave and what they value. I learned about the types of personality and skills that were requisite to engage and function with the young men so that we could accomplish the aims of the project cooperatively, such as the ability to explore oneself and try to find the common bridge that unites us despite the obvious and vast social discrepancies that exist. The aim of this project was not only to have the local adolescent be aware of the healthy environment around them and identify specific points of "health" but also to educate possible future doctors about what children from certain backgrounds find "healthy." And while I can't speak from the perspective of the local young people, I can say that in my own opinion this project was a resounding success.

Father Jim invited the youths' parents or caregivers to our last session, where they planned to make a poster presentation. Jim told us that they were very shy but that we should try to see what happens. When we arrived in the church basement that last day, we discovered that the board that we had left on the wall that had been ready for final changes had been taken down and destroyed. The CUSP students could not understand what had happened. Apparently another group that used the basement felt no respect for the work that we had done and did not know we would be back to work on it. In any case, the CUSP students and the Skills Academy students put together another presentation.

Lessons Learned

Crucial to the task of community service-learning is relationship building. I worked with Jim for many months before he and I agreed on a summer project. We established a "friendly relationship," asking each other for advice on matters that we shared. We created bonds of trust that enabled us to proceed with the work that included two different groups of young people with very different opportunity trajectories. The time investment necessary to build relationships cannot be underestimated when developing community service-learning courses and projects. Compared with preparing for a lecture, the activities and responsibilities involved in building relationships are much greater in this approach. It entails more than merely finding a suitable place for students to carry out their service activities because at stake are principles of good practice that include reciprocity and mutuality. Communities have long histories in which they become the object of academic investigation, research, and sites for course-based activities. It is not unusual for community leaders and activists to confront researchers and ask, "What are we going to get out of this?"

To allay community concerns, it is important to bring community involvement into the process as early as possible. As a project is conceptualized, it is vital to enable community partners to invest in the relationship by identifying their goals and objectives in developing the project. This may sound simpler than it is. Unless communities already have researchable goals and objectives in mind, they often have difficulty in providing concrete ideas about what they want to achieve in the relationship. I have never experienced a total rejection. However, I have endured long, seemingly unproductive meetings to discover community goals. In retrospect, such meetings are, in fact, quite productive. They are the basis for building trust through a type of humanizing process that results in a more direct, instrumental approach, usually used in contractual arrangements. Jim and I spent time discussing what a project would look like. I visited the site where his youths participated, and I interacted with them to get a sense of who they are and what it might feel like to the Cornell University students. Jim and I shared a meal or two, creating the kind of relationship that eliminates the contractual formalism that we find antithetical to the kind of relationship we wanted both groups of youths to develop.

Humanizing the process is vital to community service-learning as an anthropological project. Stanley Diamont (1974) wrote, "The anthropologist who treats the indigene as an object may define himself as relatively free and integrated, a subject, a person, but that is an illusion" (p. 402). Precisely, Diamont goes on to say that if we take seriously our attempt to understand others, we must simultaneously seek to understand ourselves by employing the same critical perspective. He stresses that, by objectifying people, we engage in a process of self-alienation and that critical self-reflection is a crucial element in community service-learning or action research.

Community service-learning is the converse of researching the *other*. It is very much about leveling the playing field and respecting what everyone brings to the table: knowledge, skills, experience, wisdom, and so on. The importance of producing knowledge (the "learning" in community service-learning) is that it is a social act. It is interactive and participatory, a mutually satisfying and beneficial interaction at a very basic human level. We do this by accepting all people "where they are at."

On a basic level, we should be seeking interdependence, not scholarly independence. To illustrate: Ralph L. Beals (1969), the former president of the American Anthropology Association, wrote in response to CIA involvement in foreign research during the Vietnam War, "To expand the theoretical and methodological bases of his discipline, the social scientist must be free from constraint in selecting problems and study methods and sharing the results of his research" (p. 2). I believe human welfare to be synonymous with social justice, which is best served when our subjects of study participate in the research project as coequals with an equal stake in the design, process, and outcome of the project.

Reducing the potential for inequalities is central to community service-learning. Inequalities are often created by academic opportunism through which funding streams define projects that are implemented in communities. In this milieu, community-based organizations may view academic expertise as a service to be hired or one that is "helping" their community. To avoid this type of reasoning, a partnership should be established with members who identify and develop projects together. Relationship development provides the context for partners to learn together. Working together will inevitably take time but will provide a firm foundation for authentic collaboration as a common goal. Part of our mutuality also resulted in the resources each of us brought to the project. Although I volunteered to buy the pizza and soda that smoothed over the interaction, Jim made it a point to fund this part of the project. We provided the cameras, processing, and other supplies.

As we have seen, service-learning outcomes are often beyond academic content in that they provide students with mechanisms for personal development. Students are able to clarify personal values. For example, most CUSP students did not have experience with people of color or with people from low-income neighborhoods. The "border-crossing" aspect of the project that I have described enhances these students' abilities to work across issues of difference. It reduces the anxieties they feel when entering new and different social fields. Through community service-learning, students appreciate the kind of learning that is only possible outside of books and lectures, involving dynamic, nonlinear, complex, and unpredictable interactions.

Finally, for some students, community service-learning is a doorway toward taking civic responsibilities in the future. Students who do not view their career aspiration as service oriented come to the realization that service is not an either-or activity. They learn the possibility of integrating civic responsibility, and service to others, as an aspect of their life-ways rather than a full-time commitment of work. For others, service-learning is a doorway exploring how their personal life-ways may incorporate service as an alternative professional path.

Postscript

On our last day with the Skills Academy students, two Cornell students broke away early from the group and walked the few blocks to the subway station. As we later learned, a man walked up the subway stairs the students were walking down and grabbed one of the student's handbag, which was slung over her shoulder. She refused to release it and struggled for it with her assailant. The other student pulled at him to get him away from her friend. In the process they rolled down the stairs with the man wrapping his teeth around the first woman's thumb, biting it hard enough to break the skin.

This struggle took place over a few minutes. At some point, as the man understood that the girls would not give in to him, he ran away. A man dressed in Hasidic garb, whom the students recognized as a member of the Orthodox Jewish community in Williamsburg, ran after the attacker. He shortly returned to the students, apologizing for not being able to catch him. The Manhattan Transport Authority (MTA) police were alerted to the situation. A 911 call brought an ambulance that sped the two women away. In the meantime, other CUSP students came upon the scene, and one had the presence of mind to call me on my cell phone. I happened to be in Father Jim's car, and both of us sped to the MTA police precinct in downtown Brooklyn where the two women had been taken to be interviewed.

While there are many more details to this story, I will end here because I want to make one more point about the impact of an asset-based approach. The two young women came from privileged white families, affluent enough to afford the cost of this relatively expensive summer program. It could have been easy enough for this event to have changed their view not only of Bed-Stuy, the people who live there, or even the Skills Academy students with whom they had interacted. Instead, they easily separated out what had happened and saw the brutal attack as a separate matter from their experiences with the youngsters. Moreover, as the CUSP students came to learn about the turn of events, they understood even more clearly the nature of disadvantage that their new young friends had to live with in their struggle to map out their futures.

Some time later, I was able to speak to some of the students in Manhattan. We discussed the dramatic way the summer session ended, and I asked them how they felt about what had happened. They needed no time to think of a response. Sean and Lauren (19 and 18 years old respectively and dating each other), Noelle (18 years old from Hong Kong), and Julia (18 years old and Jewish American) each in turn remarked that they were horrified by what had taken place, but they understood well enough to separate out the negative from positive experiences they so enjoyed with the teenagers from Bed-Stuy.

Endnotes

1) See Beck 2001, 2005, 2006.

2) Reflexivity refers to reflecting on oneself in the context of professional practice. It is like the Marxian notion of "praxis," which represents the simultaneity of theorizing and doing. This is an important skill for students to learn because it creates an ability to actively engage intellectually in the process of carrying out an activity.

3) I want to thank Marianne A. Cocchini and Joe Hall for discussions that led me to understand the significance of such a concept as it is used to theorize children under conditions of poverty and in youth development practice.

References

Beals, R. L. (1969). *Politics of social research: An inquiry into the ethics and responsibilities of social scientists.* Chicago, IL: Aldine Publishing Company.

Beck, S. (2001). Radicalizing anthropology? Toward experiential learning. *Anthropology of Work Review, 22*(2),1–6.

Beck, S. (2005). Community service learning. *General Anthropology, 12*(1–2), 1, 9–11.

Beck, S. (2006). Experiential learning, lived practice, and knowing-in-action. *Anthropology of Work Review, 26*(2).

Citizens' Committee for Children of New York City. (2005). *Keeping track of New York City's children* (7th ed.). New York, NY: Author.

CUSP Students. (2005). *Healthy Wednesdays in our hood* [Brochure]. New York, NY: Cornell University, Urban Semester Program.

Diamont, S. (1974). Anthropology in question. In D. Hymes (Ed.), *Reinventing anthropology* (pp. 401–429). New York, NY: Vintage Books.

Fanon, F. (1963). *The wretched of the earth.* New York, NY: Grove Press.

Gramsci, A. (1957). *The modern prince.* New York, NY: International Publishing Company.

Klein, A. N. (1974). Counter culture and cultural hegemony: Some notes on the youth rebellion of the 1960s. In D. Hymes (Ed.), *Reinventing anthropology* (pp. 312–334). New York, NY: Vintage Books.

Kozol, J. (2005). *The shame of the nation: The restoration of Apartheid schooling in America.* New York, NY: Crown.

Wang, C., & Burris, M. A. (1994). Empowerment through photovoice: Portraits of participation. *Health Education Quarterly, 21*(2), 171–186.

Wang, C., Wu, K., Zhan, W., & Carovano, K. (1998). Photovoice as a participatory health promotion strategy. *Health Promotion International, 13*(1), 75–86.

Youth Take Charge: Social Action in a University-Community Partnership

4

Joan Arches

The Healthy Initiative Collaborative: Community-University Partnership (Hic Cup) is an undergraduate service-learning partnership involving undergraduate students at the College of Public and Community Service (CPCS) of the University of Massachusetts–Boston (UMass–Boston) and youth from a neighboring housing development. Hic Cup developed from the desire to harness the power of community-university partnerships, participatory action research, and service-learning in order to respond to the needs of low-income youth and to elevate their voice in their community. The Hic Cup collaborative has carried out social action as it is conceived of in Europe to focus on the needs of young people and to develop youth leadership.

Social action (Flemming & Ward, 1999) builds on the work of Paulo Freire (1970). It is rooted in the belief that people of all ages and in a range of settings can take action to achieve their collectively identified goals. While decision-making is up to the participants, group workers facilitate a five-part process in which the group members identify and document what the problems are, analyze why the problems exist, determine how to arrive at an action plan, carry out the action, and continuously reflect upon the learning.

By collaborating with the UMass–Boston students to implement the social action process, the participating youth learned to identify and document problems, prioritize their needs, and assess their options for meeting those needs. After conducting the research, they selected an issue related to the lack of recreational activities for youth and together worked to create conditions to obtain a basketball park. Remaining true to the philosophy of social action, university students worked with the youth to facilitate the process. In class they carried out the practice principles of service-learning by reflecting on their actions in groups, acting as consultants for each other, and connecting theory to practice. This Hic Cup collaborative demonstrates that service-learning meets the service and technical needs of the community as well as the needs of students for learning and academic development.

Service-Learning and University-Community Partnerships

Service-learning in this context emphasizes three values: the role of experience in the learning process, the need for critical thinking as one approaches new knowledge, and the university's responsibility to its neighbors. The Hic Cup collaborative is rooted in the belief that the purpose of education is to promote the public good and that the problems of a democratic society are problems that educational institutions should be addressing (Dewey, 1916). The partnership recognized that students can contribute to—and learn from—the community.

Hic Cup incorporates theory, practice, and reflection (Eyler & Giles, 1997). In cautioning against letting service-learning become another way to exploit communities, Robert Sigmon (1979) developed three guiding principles, which have informed the work of Hic Cup. First, the population being served must control the service. Second, those being served must develop their own capacities to serve and act. Third, those who serve must be recognized as learners.

Several principles of university-community partnerships have guided this collaboration. As institutions of higher education have seen the value in institutionalizing service-learning as a way to engage with surrounding communities, university-community partnerships have evolved as a means of developing democratic, collaborative relationships with the community. They have also changed the way the university has related to its neighbors. Hic Cup has recognized that university-community partnerships provide opportunities for innovative teaching and learning while making real contributions to communities. This collaborative effort has worked to build long-term relationships through which social and political issues facing youth in the community have been addressed. The partnership has been based on activities that represent mutually agreed upon expectations, goals, and benefits for all constituents. The patterns of interaction and relationships reflect the acknowledgement that not only does the university have resources that are of value to the community but that the community offers the university valuable opportunities for learning and creating knowledge. Committed to the concept of civic responsibility and the benefits of civic engagement, our partnership reflects the university's commitment to provide educational opportunities and research focused on addressing the needs and concerns of the communities in which it is located. Addressing the fundamental questions raised by Dewey about education for whom and for what, this partnership works to support the notion that higher education institutions must assume approaches that encourage community building and community development as they reconnect education to society (Dewey, 1902).

Theoretical Perspectives

The principles of positive youth development that underlie this collaborative project reflect the belief that young people need support and opportunities from adults in their families, schools, and communities in order to develop into successful adults. As we partner with youth at the local level, youth development has included trying to build a community where young people are respected, valued as partners, and participate actively in decision-making (Delgado, 2002). As they have developed skills, and as the opportunities to use them have unfolded, the youth have gained confidence and felt empowered. The youth felt better about themselves as they served and made a difference in their community, and in turn, negative community perceptions about youth have changed (Ginwright & James, 2002). Nonformal learning takes place in a safe, caring atmosphere, where there are ample opportunities to successfully build skills supporting positive youth development and transformational leadership (van Linden & Fertman, 1998).

Youth Leadership

The youth leadership model the class applied is based on transformational and transactional leadership with youth, as put forth by van Linden and Fertman (1998). The model assumes that all youth have the potential to become leaders in school, in the workplace, in their families, and in their communities. The young people and the students have learned about and developed their own leadership by engaging in activities in which they define leadership and communication skills, start to change their attitude toward leadership, identify different models of decision-making, and work on ways to identify and address stress.

This type of leadership emphasizes the importance of young people thinking for themselves, communicating their thoughts and feelings, helping others to act positively on their beliefs, and engaging in socially responsible activities (van Linden & Fertman, 1998, p. 17).

Social Action

Hic Cup aims to promote youth leadership through positive development and participation grounded in social action and self-directed groupwork. *Social action* is a values-based practice, informed by six principles. The principles emphasize social justice, the rights of people to define their own problems and act on their own behalf, the power of collective action, identifying social and economic aspects of what appear to be individual problems, and workers acting in a nonelitist manner ("The Impact of Social Action," 2001).

The social action methodology, like participatory action research, requires a change in the traditional role of the professional worker from that of the expert giving advice, leading, and directing to working as a partner by listening, posing questions, facilitating, supporting action, and encouraging reflection (Flemming & Ward, 1999). The power to make decisions is always with those who will be directly affected by the outcome. Users of services and community residents formulate and direct all projects. Workers come together as a team and meet regularly with a consultant who facilitates a nonhierarchical process of discussion, with time to allow for learning through reflection and problem posing.

Self-directed groupwork (Mullender & Ward, 1991) is the practice method by which social action is carried out. It can be applied to groups working for social change in a variety of settings. In addition to the values base and five-part process of social action, Mullender and Ward identify five stages in this model. In the *pre-planning*, or stage A, the team is assembled and clarifies its values. Also before meeting the youth, the students spend time in class discussing values and approaches to working with youth. Stage B, or *group takes off*, establishes guidelines and starts the process of defining the issue. Each semester the youth decide upon rules and guidelines that the group will follow. In stage C, the *group prepares to take action*, workers facilitate the process of deciding which issue the group will address, analyzing root causes, and identifying an action plan. Although Hic Cup members decided to work on a basketball court, there were many short-term projects and decisions to undertake to get to their ultimate goal. It is in stage D that the *group takes action*. Stage E is characterized as the *group takes charge*, in which the group works on the issue while reflecting on the process.

These stages are not purely linear, and with each obstacle the new student groups face, they find themselves at an earlier stage. The youth leadership approach to positive youth development fits within the process of social action and self-directed groupwork. Each semester youth leaders emerge to move the group forward and assist new university students. Together they embrace developing skills for social change, providing opportunities for marginalized youth to build community by analyzing and acting on an understanding of the impact of political, social, and economic factors on their lives. The methods of social action and self-directed groupwork build on participatory action research (Sarri & Sarri, 1992) and other methodologies that have been successful in projects that recognize youth as resources and active participants (Finn & Checkoway, 1998).

Social action and youth leadership lend themselves to service-learning pedagogy. This approach to teaching and learning finds its roots in early educational philosophical writings. Dewey (1916) argued that communities should be integrally connected to education by providing forums for knowledge to be acted upon and by advancing the student's as well as the community's interest. More recently, through the work of such organizations as Campus Compact—a national organization representing presidents of colleges and universities devoted to engaged learning—and the National Service-Learning Clearinghouse, service-learning is recognized for its relevance in promoting civic engagement and responding to the needs of individuals and communities.

The Community

The housing development of Harbor Point is the University of Massachusetts–Boston's closest urban neighbor on the peninsula of Columbia Point. Currently, there are approximately 2,800 residents living in Harbor Point housing, with 30% of the units allotted to low-income residents. This means that of the 1,262 households, 400 are low income. The majority of the 600 children under age 18 at Harbor Point live with low-income families. There are 372 youth between the ages of 11 and 18. Fifty percent of the youth are identified as black, 22% are Hispanic, 18% are white, and 10% are Asian.

In 1993 the Columbia Point Coalition, an association of businesses and service providers affiliated with the peninsula, conducted a needs assessment in which concerns of youth were identified as one of six major needs of the community. The coalition recommended giving youth a greater voice in the housing development and initiating university-community partnerships to build community, including opportunities for youth. These findings were confirmed in a needs assessment published in a 1999 report, *Building Community*, conducted by the UMass–Boston service-learning collaborative (Arches & Aponte-Pares, 1999).

The UMass–Boston collaborative investigated past and present programs and initiatives offered by the university to Harbor Point residents and identified needs of the residents. After conducting focus groups and

individual interviews, they concluded that the needs of youth were largely going unmet and that the youth voice was not being heard. The
Building Community report of this collaborative cited that every constituency and community partner on Columbia Point listed youth programs as a need (Arches & Aponte-Pares, 1999). Youth referred to their
negative image on the peninsula and in the larger community. They felt
there was no place to hang out and that most recreational facilities on the
point were off limits to them. One of the only options for fun, as they
saw it, was to harass pedestrians. Various adult constituencies voiced concern about gangs, drugs, and lack of opportunities for young people.

These findings were upheld in fall 2002 at a visioning meeting of the
now-defunct Columbia Point Community Partnership. Once again, youth
issues and needs were listed among the top five priorities. Although the
community always had a youth center, internal difficulties and its reliance
on soft money made its scope and ability to serve a wide range of youth
very limited. In the months before the Hic Cup collaborative began, the
youth center was closed, and a process of finding new management was
underway. The center reopened two months after the beginning of Hic
Cup. Since then Hic Cup has maintained communication and partnership
activities with the center's director, who is a resident of the community.

The Process and the Project

All of the youth involved in Hic Cup were living in low-income resi-
dences. A trusted youth worker recruited youth at the on-site community health center who were likely to benefit from a group experience that
would provide an opportunity to build social and interpersonal skills.
They have met once a week for 90 minutes since 2003. They originally
joined the project to get involved in their communities and become community leaders. As part of the process, they learned to become community researchers, documenting the pros and cons of community life for
young people at Harbor Point housing and mapping their concerns.
They designed surveys and interviews and conducted data analysis. As
the first semester ended, the group who named themselves HPCRU

(Harbor Point Community Research Unit) decided that the major action project would be to develop a basketball park.

The College of Public and Community Service students are a mixed-gender, multicultural group of adults between 21 and 50. Each semester approximately half of the students continue on with the project as part of their capstone requirement, and the other half are replaced by a new group. They meet with the youth in a group at the health center and then return to class to process what happened in light of the theories and readings they have been assigned and to serve as consultants to each other with the professor. In class the professor guides them through reflections and provides feedback on their experience that evening. The professor also engages them in discussion about a related theoretical framework for the field of youth-work practice, group work, social action, and community transformation. Each week after they have read their assignments, they write a reflection paper on what they did in group, what they read, and how the readings might help with what they are doing with the youth. Recognizing the importance of meaningful participation, the objectives of the work with the youth are to support youth input in the decision-making affecting their lives, to encourage their voices as agents of community change, and to help them learn skills that will enable them to understand how the social systems in their environment work.

Too often, youth—particularly low-income youth of color—feel that they are at the mercy of forces outside their control and that their options for positive behavior are limited. They may be unaware of the actual rules in effect at their housing development or in school and that there are structural ways to change those rules. Once the youth learn about the power structure and the policies that operate in their surroundings, they can participate more effectively. They can try to change those policies that limit their choices for positive activities. The students learn theories of social change and youth participation that allow them to support these objectives.

Each week the university students and the youth group open their discussion session with age-appropriate icebreakers designed to build on the stages of group development, address the developmental issues of the youth involved, and promote positive participation. This is followed by a review of prior learning, a new activity, reflection, and evaluation.

The objectives of the early meetings each semester are to get acquainted and to encourage the youth to think about themselves and their community. Recognizing the ambivalence with which the group approached the first meeting, we started off in a nonthreatening and open manner geared toward feeling comfortable and learning about each other. In the beginning youth introduced themselves and completed the sentence, "I am . . . " This was intended to give us baseline data about how the youth thought and described themselves. The university students did the same. Answers by the youth tended to be short and limited. "I am an athlete" or "a sister" or "an aunt." Each semester our first meetings encourage engagement and relationship building. Icebreakers are carefully planned to respect the youth's feeling of caution in meeting new people. The group may start with each person saying his or her name, where it comes from, or something about himself or herself that one would not know by looking at him or her.

The meetings always begin with an icebreaker that builds on what we know about the stages of group development. Building trust, engagement, and limited self-disclosure informed the early icebreakers. One icebreaker designed by the UMass–Boston students was a form of interpersonal bingo in which the youth and adults had to fill in boxes on their cards by going up to each other and asking certain questions. Each box contained an attribute, such as "speaks a language other than English." Once the person finds someone with the attribute they are looking for, they can initial that box.

Social action encourages participants to set their own guidelines and rules. Thus, early in each semester during a meeting, the goal is established to set the norms and expectations by which the group will function. Through this process, the youth voice can be heard and used to guide the project. As we began the project, the youth identified good and bad experiences they had had in groups. Based on their discussion of past experiences, they came up with a group contract, which covered norms for behavior and group expectations. Mullender and Ward (1991) refer to this stage as the "the group takes off."

The students prepared the youth for the group to take action by engaging them in a process whereby they would set their agenda, define the issues, analyze root causes, and agree upon an action plan. In one meeting the youth had an icebreaker in which they talked about where they would like to travel. This helped them think about what makes a place a good one in which to live.

Then they began to hone their skills, identifying "What is the problem?" by pretending they were documentary filmmakers who had just filmed their community ("Centre Launches Good Practice Guide," 2000). Their task in small groups with college students was to create a poster that advertised their hypothetical film. The poster had to include everything that would be in such a film and a title. The poster titles included: "Too many rules at the pool," "Nothing in the parks for kids," "The store is too expensive," and "There is too much trash." When they finished their posters, each group presented it to the rest of the group followed by questions and answers. This generated discussion about youth being bored, being treated badly by security guards when they just hang out, and having nothing to do. For example, they cited the lack of basketball hoops in the community.

The youth are in school all day and then meet in a room that does not allow a great deal of physical movement. The icebreakers are geared to take the need for kinetic action into account. For example, one meeting began with an icebreaker that encouraged movement and creativity. It was called "mime the lie." Each person had to mime an activity. When they were asked by the person sitting next to them what they were doing, they had to lie and name a different activity. The next person would then mime their lie and this continued going around the room. This allowed them to move, laugh, enjoy each other's company, and think creatively.

Having defined the problem, the youth began to focus on documentation. We had talked about what they thought were problems. Now they were going to document those problems. The youth and the university students walked around the community with disposable cameras. They took pictures and mapped what they liked and did not like about their community ("The Impact of Social Action," 2001).

The next meeting began with a student-designed icebreaker in which the youth all contributed sentences to a story describing their community. With the photos taken the previous week the youth created posters and maps of their community. When they were finished, they discussed them and added to their list of answers to "What do I like and what do

I want to change in my community?" By now trash, the need for better parks, and issues of harassment by security were coming up repeatedly, as well as the need for more general recreational activities. Out of this meeting came the decision to participate in activities which involved cleaning up the community.

Another meeting began with an icebreaker in which the youth and university students talked about their role models or people they looked up to. This was followed by a discussion of role models and leaders, and a review of what we had learned so far. It enabled them to think about leadership in different ways. Then the youth went around the room and stated what they were learning. Statements included, "I am learning how to help my community," "I am learning how be a community researcher," and "I am learning to make a difference." We agreed that they were learning how to identify what was a problem, how to obtain evidence about these problems, and how to collect data. We discussed what ways one can collect data such as through taking pictures. This led to the creation of a list of data-gathering methods, which included gathering information from surveys and interviews. The group discussed interviewing and broke into small groups to design surveys, which they shared with each other. Each group then selected two questions for a final questionnaire.

Another week began with an icebreaker in which they had to interview each other and present their findings to the group. That helped to develop listening and presentation skills, improve their observational techniques, and generally improve communication skills. They practiced social action and developed their leadership skills at the same time. They then drew maps of the community, identified where different youth hang out, and came up with a strategy for administering the questionnaires.

The following week the icebreaker focused on observation skills. Youth and mentors broke up in two groups and interviewed each other, then separated and physically changed one thing about their appearance. When they came back together, they had to notice what the change was. They reported back and talked about the importance of observation skills for community researchers. This was followed by role-plays and administering the surveys. The discussion that followed was about good and bad ways to approach people and how to explain what you are doing. They then went out in small groups and administered the questionnaires.

Another icebreaker was to count the number of times the letter "f" occurs in the phrase, "Fairness is the final result of years of effective effort combined with the experience of diversity," for which the "f" count ranged from 6–11. This led to a discussion about how people may differ in the way they respond to the same thing (Arches, 2001). The discussion demonstrated the importance of observation skills and that people may see the same thing in different ways. Then they analyzed data from questionnaires. In small groups they discussed why this was important. Among the students' comments were, "This tells us if others think the same way we do," and, "It tells us what others think." They added, "It tells us who agrees with us and who doesn't." As the youth discussed the findings, they applied concepts from math and science. They talked about the mean, median, and mode as they examined pie charts.

Adhering to the second stage of the process of social action, the UMass–Boston students initiated a discussion of why the major findings existed. The purpose of this was to look at the structural causes of the problems and to think about analyzing before deciding what should be done. The discussion focused on why security guards treat the youth poorly; their comments included, "They are racist," "They judge us all the same based on our clothes and our age," and, "They think we are all alike." In addition the students said, "They are jealous," and, "They don't understand us." Others added, "They are told to treat us this way," "It is their job," and, "Some kids do bad things."

At this meeting the youth agreed on a name, HPCRU (Harbor Point Community Research Unit). This helped to solidify the group's identity and allowed their smooth transition to the next stage of group development. They were ready to work. They entered the stage of self-directed groupwork in which the group takes action. During the meeting time was devoted to talking about a community cleanup day that was sponsored by UMass–Boston. The group talked about what area they wanted to clean up and who would be there. The community cleanup went off without a hitch, and all 12 youths participated and brought friends. The youth made posters with their new name and seemed to feel really good about it.

As the first semester came to a close, HPCRU completed their discussions about why problems exist, generated a list of possible solutions, and applied field analysis ("The Impact of Social Action," 2001) to select their issue: getting a basketball hoop or court. They agreed to work on this when we resumed as a group the next semester.

When the group resumed in the fall, there were three new CPCS students in addition to those returning from the spring semester to work with the youth and complete their capstone. The plan for the semester was to design an action plan and implement their change project: a basketball court.

Each meeting started with a developmentally appropriate icebreaker. Because we had been together for more than one semester, we delved into identity issues, moral development, and values. This first meeting began with a discussion of the question "What do I like and dislike about being a young person?" Next we discussed the composition of the group, because many new youths were involved. The youth from the previous year discussed the pros and cons of new members joining at this point and came up with a plan that basically limited the group to members who had been involved already or who were related to those who had been involved. For logistical reasons (baby-sitting obligations of older siblings for younger ones) it made sense to keep the group the same but to allow siblings to join.

Although self-directed groupwork does not encourage limiting the size of the group, we decided to honor the principle that youth have the right to define membership (Mullender & Ward, 1991). We asked questions, made sure they had sufficient information to arrive at an informed decision, and then let them make their own choices.

As they had the previous semester, the group then went about setting the norms and guidelines for participation and the rules for the meetings. As meetings could get loud and boisterous, it was important to have the group own the norms by which they would govern themselves. The third session that semester was spent creating these guidelines, reviewing what had already been learned, and setting an agenda for the semester. We recognized the importance of moral development and developed an icebreaker in which youth prioritized their top three values from a long list of possibilities. They included being with family, having leisure time, helping others, making money, having friends, and doing well in school.

This brought forth some interesting discussion and clarity about what was important for the youth involved.

The next several weeks were spent carrying out the action plan as the youth divided up into teams to work on a petition, a poem, and a proposal for the basketball court. They dedicated a substantial amount of time to role-playing and discussing communication skills in preparation for the actual petitioning. They also spent time in all sessions discussing the way decisions were made at Harbor Point and learning how to influence the process. This included identifying stakeholders, meeting the executive director of the Tenants Task Force, going out into the community, and talking to people about the governance structure.

A few sessions were spent practicing presentation skills for the proposal presentation to the task force. The youth had planned to make their presentation at the end of the semester, but a major crisis within the task force interrupted the planned agenda. As the semester drew to a close, the youth submitted their proposal in writing to the task force and presented their poem at the end-of-semester recognition event at UMass–Boston.

The third semester of the Hic Cup project began with the original 12 youths. However, this number grew to 25 by the end of the semester. Only one of the original UMass–Boston students was still with the group, and new UMass–Boston students joined the project to work on youth work practice competencies. This delayed progress as the UMass–Boston students learned the social action process and the youth established relationships with a new group. Although we had spent several weeks at the end of the previous semester discussing termination issues and feelings about the students who were leaving, it still came as a shock to the youth to have so many new faces the third semester. This is something that we have experienced every semester since then as well. We prepared for this and asked each group to write letters of introduction to each other. The first icebreaker of the new semester consisted of the youth and CPCS students engaging in one-on-one interviews and sharing the letters. The group dynamics changed significantly. We went back to issues of power and control with lots of testing behaviors. At the end of these meetings the youth decided they needed to show improvement in the areas of respect, getting along better with each other, not interrupting when others speak, raising their hands to talk, and adhering to a "three strikes" policy about breaking the rules and guidelines. The next meetings were spent codifying the guidelines in greater detail. The youth shared with the UMass–Boston students what they had learned over the past year and started to move forward on their action plan. They focused on details such as what the plan was, what their role was, what the hours would be, and how different ages would participate.

At one gathering we attempted to get into issues of diversity for the icebreaker and made use of a culture walk. In this activity the youth were read a word from a list of attributes (e.g., Latino) that could describe a group to which they belonged. They were told that if they were a member of the group, or if they identified with that group, to go to the other side of the room, face the rest of the group and say three things. First, they said one thing that they wanted people to know about the group. Second, they said one thing they never wanted to hear again about their group. Third, they said one thing they wanted from people who say they support them. This exercise did not work and elicited very little participation. In retrospect, it was clear that with the unfamiliarity of all the new UMass–Boston students, the group went back to an earlier developmental stage. We were not yet ready to engage in such serious self-disclosure. We moved ahead a bit more slowly to gain trust and establish rapport. We reviewed the decision-making process for getting the approval for the basketball court. A discussion of stakeholders and their power ensued.

Hic Cup spent a few weeks role-playing, planning a petitioning strategy, and petitioning. The youth enjoyed getting out, meeting people, and actively getting involved in the project. Over the course of this project, however, they became somewhat frustrated that their goals had not yet materialized. They had good discussions of where we were and what needed to happen, raising concerns that some of the group members were not taking the group seriously. After a change in tenant leadership, HPCRU made a presentation to the task force again to obtain their approval of the basketball court. They had 400 signatures on petitions and a completed proposal. They moved forward in the group development to the stage in which the group takes charge.

As we entered the third year, we still went through the stages of group development that accompany the introduction of new students and assisting the youth in the next stage of leadership. We have seen growth and development in all the youth. The end-of-semester evaluations, which the youth completed, yielded insights into how valuable the group was to them. Nonetheless, because there had been so many changes in the adult leadership in the organizations involved in building the basketball court, the goals had still not been realized. This has caused problems of trust in general and a reluctance to believe that youth can really make a difference. At this point, the youth were more interested in coming together to socialize, as the impact of learned helplessness developed. They were frustrated that it had taken so long and that their goals did not come to fruition. They questioned whether they could really change systems and whether they should even try.

This has presented the group members with challenges that they continue to address while they fundraise and work on activities that still reflect their original goals. At times, the youth's lack of enthusiasm and refusal to move along with the process caused frustration and despair with the university students.

Conclusions

Based on the theory of social action and self-directed groupwork, the youth have learned skills in community research. They can now think about their community and how it meets their needs by drawing pictures, walking around, mapping the issues, and documenting the problems they encounter. They have learned to design and administer surveys and analyze data using basic math concepts. Their learning process has included analytical thinking and getting to root causes of problems by asking, "Why?"

Building on youth leadership principles and positive youth development, the youth have improved their communication skills and have developed interviewing and observational skills. Throughout this process they learned to make their voices heard. They discovered how they can use academic work to enhance their lives. By working in a supportive environment with adults who respected them and listened to what they had to say, they built on their strengths and developed leadership skills while engaging with their community.

The service-learning and university-community partnership components of Hic Cup positively influenced the UMass–Boston students who reported back that while they had never worked so hard, they also had never learned so much. They developed skills in planning events and deepened their substantive and theoretical knowledge about youth, social systems, communities, and community building. Some of the CPCS students presented their work at conferences, and others participated in community meetings, university forums, and youth work classes.

The amount of work and the difficulty of working for social change frustrated both the students and the youth. Some came to class positively drained. But by the end of each semester, most of the students changed the way they viewed young people and the community. They developed skills in working with youth and communities. By learning about and applying social action, the students found meaningful roles as partners in community social change.

References

Arches, J. (2001). Powerful partnerships. *Journal of Community Practice, 9*(2), 15–30.

Arches, J., & Aponte-Pares, L. (1999). *Building community.* Boston, MA: University of Massachusetts–Boston, Office of the Chancellor.

Centre launches good practice guide. (2000, September). *Centre for Social Action Newsletter, 2,* 1–4.

Delgado, M. (2002). *New frontiers for youth development in the twenty-first century: Revitalizing and broadening youth development.* New York, NY: Columbia University Press.

Dewey, J. (1902). The school as social centre. *Elementary School Teacher, 3*(2), 73–86.

Dewey, J. (1916). *Democracy and education.* New York, NY: Macmillan.

Eyler, J., & Giles, D., Jr. (1997). The importance of program quality in service-learning. In A. S. Waterman (Ed.), *Service-learning: Applications from the research* (pp. 57–76). Mahwah, NJ: Lawrence Erlbaum Associates.

Finn, J. L., & Checkoway, B. (1998). Young people as competent community builders: A challenge to social work. *Social Work, 43*(4), 335–345.

Flemming, J., & Ward, D. (1999). Research as empowerment: The social action approach. In W. Shera & L. M. Wells (Eds.), *Empowerment practice in social work: Developing richer conceptual frameworks* (pp. 371–389). Toronto, Canada: Canadian Scholars' Press.

Freire, P. (1970). *Pedagogy of the oppressed.* New York, NY: Continuum.

Ginwright, S., & James, T. (2002, Winter). From assets to agents of change: Social justice, organizing and youth development. *New Directions for Youth Development, 96,* 27–46.

The impact of social action—20 years on the Ainsley teenage action group. (2001, January). *Centre for Social Action Newsletter, 3,* 1–3.

Mullender, A., & Ward, D. (1991). *Self-directed groupwork: Users take action for empowerment.* London, England: Whiting & Birch.

Sarri, R. C., & Sarri, C. M. (1992). Organizational and community change through participatory action research. *Administration in Social Work, 16*(3/4), 99–122.

Sigmon, R. (1979). Service-learning: Three principles. *Synergist, 8,* 9–11.

van Linden, J., & Fertman, C. (1998). *Youth leadership: A guide to understanding leadership development in adolescents.* San Francisco, CA: Jossey-Bass.

Practicing Active Learning: Introducing Urban Geography and Engaging Community in Pilsen, Chicago

5

Winifred Curran, Euan Hague, Harpreet Gill

In order to foster a sense of civic engagement in our students, we designed an introductory urban geography course as a community-based service-learning course (CbSL) at DePaul University in Chicago. The course introduced students to the development of the American city. Students collected visual and archival data on buildings for the Pilsen Alliance, a community-based organization in Pilsen, a largely Mexican American neighborhood close to downtown Chicago. The student-collected data will be used to control development in Pilsen, which is currently threatened by gentrification.

Community-Based Service-learning

The word "community" is fraught with contradictions, and its definitions may be as much about exclusion as about democracy. CbSL must be specific about meaningful education, democratic processes, and the commitment to disadvantaged communities by existing social, political, and economic arrangements. That said, universities are frequently seen as disconnected from the so-called real world and from local communities and community-based institutions. Although academics have popularly been envisioned as living in an ivory tower, they have aimed to correct

79

this outdated view of academe through their work with community-based research and CbSL.

The goals of CbSL are indeed lofty. Accomplishing its ideals of generating critical, responsible, active citizens, an engaged academic institution, and a multicultural, democratic, progressive community is difficult. As Cone and Harris (1996) recognized, "multicultural experiences do not necessarily lead to a 'multicultural attitude' (i.e., one that is tolerant and understanding) . . . simply experiencing new worlds doesn't necessarily increase understanding and may even serve to confirm stereotyped perspectives" (p. 32). Ensuring that CbSL becomes a transformative experience for students and useful to local communities is an enormous responsibility for faculty and their supporting institutions.

The Urban Context of Gentrification

As an urban university DePaul finds itself an active participant in some of the social politics issues students experience in our urban geography course. Perhaps the most explosive of these issues is gentrification: the influx of upper-income residents into a previously working-class area. This results in the displacement of the working class, immigrants, and communities of color. Gentrification is remaking the American city in several ways. It changes the physical appearance of the city as gentrifiers rehabilitate old buildings and construct new ones, start new businesses, and demand more urban services. It also impacts the composition of the population as high-income professionals who are primarily white move in.

The study of gentrification is pedagogically rich and fundamentally connected to other urban social politics such as segregation, deindustrialization, urban renewal, suburbanization, crime, and urban governance, as well as globalization, immigration, and the nature of community. Students can easily observe urban landscapes and the social politics that surround them in their everyday experiences of Chicago. In order to discuss gentrification, we must explain the history of the American city and examine how cities work. Once students understand the historical context in which gentrification occurs, they are able to draw upon their own experiences of gentrification and generate discussions and develop a deeper understanding of the consequences of this issue.

One of our classroom strategies has been to teach gentrification by utilizing Neil Smith's influential rent gap thesis (Smith, 1996). The rent gap is the difference between actual and potential ground rent. In other words, as certain areas of the city have been devalued, land values become less expensive than they could have been given locational advantages such as proximity to the financial district and access to public transportation. Since the mid 1960s, urban neighborhoods in the U.S. that experienced rent gaps have tended to be located in inner city areas, which usually house the working classes and minority populations. These areas became attractive for gentrification because of their central location to social and cultural amenities and because of the real estate value, which was far less than existing upper-income neighborhoods.

Once students understand the rent gap concept, we explain how rent gaps came into existence by asking: Why do certain neighborhoods become *bad* neighborhoods, and why are large sections of the city in need of revitalization? This leads us back to the Chicago school and its model of the city identified by Davis (1998) as "the most famous diagram in social science" (p. 364). This was a model where different populations resided in different concentric zones surrounding a central business district. Those who needed to live close to work, such as the working classes, lived in central areas of the city. Those who could afford to commute tended to live away from the negative externalities associated with the industrial city.

Historical processes that generate rent gaps have relied on disinvestment and racial segregation, which was fortified by the emergence of suburban development (Jackson, 1985). After World War II the federal government funneled millions of dollars into supporting inexpensive mortgages in the suburbs for the white middle classes. This left the inner cities with very little federal support. Federal highway construction also served to undermine the urban core. As its population shifted from the core to the suburbs, so too did jobs. Since the 1960s deindustrialization has hit cities in the U.S. (primarily the Northern states) particularly hard. Employers moved manufacturing jobs to the suburbs, to the Sunbelt, and overseas in search of cheaper and nonunion labor. Industrial neighborhoods in the central city became largely abandoned from the loss of jobs and population, contributing to urban blight. During this period federal and urban governments tried to regenerate such areas through urban renewal policies that tore down entire neighborhoods. Many of these areas were rebuilt as massive public housing projects that became warehouses for the poor and emblematic of urban poverty like the slums they replaced (Curran, 2001; Gans, 1962; Jacobs, 1961).

With the declining tax base due to the loss of population and jobs, cities experienced fiscal crises that resulted in severe budget cuts, loss of social services, and a decline in urban infrastructure, including public transportation and road maintenance. Certain neighborhoods were strategically abandoned through policies of planned shrinkage (Curran, 2001). Law enforcement, sanitation, health care, and education were cut, and as a result crime often soared. By the late 1960s major U.S. cities, Chicago included, had terrible reputations, and the value of their urban real estate plummeted. Inner city neighborhoods were redlined,[1] and residents could not afford to keep up their houses. Abandonment and arson became widespread (Marcuse, 1986).

Fiscal retrenchment and supply-side economics, most famously associated with the late President Ronald Reagan's administration, led urban governments to shift their focus from social services and industrial job retention to entrepreneurial activities. They attempted to attract multinational corporations and the high-income jobs that accompany them (Harvey, 1989). Tax credits, public-private partnerships, and other financial packages such as Tax Increment Financing (TIF) and Empowerment Zones formed the backbone of policies aimed at urban revitalization and gentrification (McCarthy, 1999). These policies were further fortified by the globalization of the economy, which made certain cities more attractive for capital investment than others. Inner-city neighborhoods with distinctive architectural styles, such as brownstones and industrial-style lofts, were rediscovered by gentrifiers. The upper-income and white-collar workers were attracted to the centrality of urban living and the growing numbers of jobs in finance, high technology, telecommunications, and other such sectors. As white-collar workers demanded more entertainment, restaurants, bars, and other amenities, low-paying service jobs were created and filled by members of a growing immigrant community.

Urban universities in this context are frequently catalysts for gentri-fication. They push land values higher, attracting upper-income popula-tions and advocating for policing strategies that will make their privileged students feel safe in the urban environment. DePaul University is no exception. It is located in the Lincoln Park neighborhood of Chicago, an area that was largely Puerto Rican before gentrification efforts turned it into one of the city's most expensive neighborhoods (Cruz, 2004). DePaul students generally have no idea about the history of the neigh-borhood in which they live and study. The transformation of Lincoln Park serves as an example of what happens when a university, proud of its commitment to social justice, is the catalyst for gentrification. Today DePaul aims to keep the promise of its commitment to social justice by giving back to the community, even though it had a role in displacing the old predominantly Puerto Rican community. Alejandra Ibañez, the director of the Pilsen Alliance, stated that DePaul became involved in ser-vice-learning projects in Pilsen because, "DePaul owes the Latino com-munity."

Pilsen

The neighborhood of Pilsen, approximately three miles southwest of Chicago's downtown loop, has been part of Chicago since the city's incor-poration in 1837 (Adelman, 1983). The area has a housing stock that dates back to the neighborhood's inception in the 1880s and 1890s as the port of entry for Central and Eastern European immigrants. Since the 1950s the area has become a major center of Latino population, primar-ily Mexican American. According to the 2000 Census, Pilsen is 88.9% Latino, and 49.1% of its neighborhood population is foreign-born. The median income per household is $27,763, about $10,000 below the City of Chicago median household income (Pilsen Alliance, 2005).

Its proximity to the downtown commercial district, old buildings, and relatively low rents resulted in Pilsen becoming ripe for gentrifica-tion. Chicago has seen a boom in the real estate market, with condo-minium developments at the forefront. The Pilsen Alliance notes that house prices have risen an average of 68% between 1990 and 2000 (Pilsen Alliance, 2005).

These changes led to extensive community organizing and resistance. The Pilsen Alliance formed in 1998, with gentrification as one of its primary concerns: "Local leaders are concerned that surrounding high-end development will result in loss of jobs, affordable housing, and displace existing residents and businesses" (Pilsen Alliance, 2004, p. 1).

The Development of a Community Mapping Project

The introductory urban geography class at DePaul University fulfilled the experiential learning requirement for junior year students. The classroom-based section of the course and the CbSL field-based section ran parallel, so that when study topics such as gentrification, industrial restructuring, or architecture were examined through lecture and readings, students could draw on their field experience to enhance their understanding of the materials being presented.

The Steans Center for Community-based Service Learning, which is DePaul University's on-site institution to support such projects, put the course together. Faculty members in the geography department met with community organizers in the Pilsen Alliance in early 2003 to plan a project that could be mutually beneficial. The project was designed to engage undergraduate students in active learning by demonstrating the complexities of urban land use patterns, gentrification, and development control through the use of zoning and TIF regulations. The Pilsen Alliance, in turn, was particularly concerned with the impact of TIF on the neighborhood. Using ArcGIS, a specific computer software, maps were printed out that identified the properties inside and outside the Pilsen TIF district. They centered on an area in the northeast of Pilsen, closest to downtown, which community organizers feared was most susceptible to gentrification and the displacement of Latino residents. In January 2004 about eight months after our planning for the project commenced, students were divided into groups of four to survey a four-block area that contained properties within and outside the TIF district. In addition, the students collected historical and visual information.

Student Reactions, Project Outcomes, and Problems

It was difficult to gauge student reaction to this initial iteration of the CbSL project in Pilsen, because there was no formal process of guided reflection or discussion about student experiences and observations. This is a process that in time was added. As a result, the best indicators of student reactions came from anonymous course evaluations at the end of the academic year. Many students expressed positive experiences. One wrote that it "helped me open my eyes to the world around me." Others reacted negatively to the course content with comments such as, "awful, very dangerous and unhealthy." Student comments were helpful in reformulating the project. They made suggestions such as, "Narrow the spectrum of what the project should be about." One student explained that it was "hard to decide what was important." Another added, "The goals of the [Pilsen Alliance] need to be more specific." All of these comments helped us redefine the course.

Further discussions with students highlighted major problems. The first problem was the repetitive nature of the historical descriptions that students were required to document. These data were of little use to the Pilsen Alliance, particularly because the information that the students presented was mostly descriptive and as a result did not allow easy visualization and explanation of existing trends in Pilsen. Collection of the data also proved to be inconsistent. This was at least in part the result of a lack of systematic oversight.

Course Redesign: Community Mapping

If the somewhat disappointing results of the first iteration of the CbSL project revealed anything, it was that all parties were encouraged to continue. The TIF district had not emerged as a critical factor in determining shifts in property taxes. Instead, the zoning status appeared, on review of the materials collected by students, to be a driving force in inflating property values in Pilsen. It was clear that the project needed rethinking. Re-visioning the project began during discussions at a number of regional conferences (Hague, 2004a, 2004b). Concurrently, the Pilsen Alliance had chosen to pursue the formation of a community zoning board. They demanded to be alerted about and to be permitted to review applications for zoning changes that had been made to the City of Chicago's Committee on Zoning. It was evident that the second iteration of the CbSL project would use zoning as a major focus. This belief was reinforced in March 2004 when the Pilsen Alliance successfully passed a ballot initiative. They gained close to 95% support for the question, "Shall the alderman hold open public meetings on zoning changes in Pilsen?" A 19-member Pilsen Community Zoning Board was established on November 15, 2004 (Kim, 2004). After discussions, academic and community participants realized that what was necessary for maintaining a vigilant outlook for real estate development was a comprehensive database of existing property and zoning status in the neighborhood. The decision was made to undertake an extensive and systematic community-mapping project in order to produce a database of the building conditions. The aim was to make information on building permits, property taxes, assessed values, property sales, and ownership publicly available.[2]

Running the Community Mapping Project

The community-mapping project in its most recent version ran in three stages. First, students were given a directed walking tour around Pilsen. This required students to answer questions en route about the neighborhood and what they saw. It was like an academic scavenger hunt in which the students wrote about how Pilsen is undergoing development pressures.[3] Second, the project required students to find and use five recently published articles about Pilsen in the *Chicago Tribune*. Incorporating field experience and archival research helped students to identify ongoing debates about land use and development in Pilsen.

Students met with politically active residents who opposed gentrification, and with property owners who were encouraged by rising property values and hoped the trend would continue.[4] After their initial walking tour, students were instructed on how to use publicly available databases to gain property ownership and taxation information. Blank surveys were distributed to the students, and each student was assigned to survey a one-to two-block area of Pilsen, about 50 buildings. A lengthy PowerPoint presentation of 50 slides was prepared in conjunction with The Resurrection Project (TRP) and the University of Illinois at Chicago (UIC). It instructed the students on how to assess individual properties. The survey was divided into two main sections. First, students were required to complete visual inspections of buildings within their designated area, evaluating their condition as poor, fair, or good. They also noted other features, such as building height, the condition of sidewalks, and other similar factors. This part of the project was largely completed without problems. The second section of the survey directed students to web sites of the City of Chicago and Cook County to discover information about property taxation, zoning laws, building permits, house sales, and assessed values. It was at this stage that we encountered numerous student questions asking where the information they needed was located on a web site or what data they should be recording.

For the final stage of the project students were given guidance on how to use simple descriptive statistics to summarize the data that they had collected and on how to write about their designated areas. They evaluated the potential impact of future development. Students were advised that their data, evaluations, and recommendations for their blocks might be used by the Pilsen Alliance. They planned a series of community meetings designed to help residents come up with a community plan that articulates a different vision for Pilsen. This was a vision with room for the working-class immigrant community that has built the neighborhood.

Reflection

Guided reflection is essential to evaluating the effectiveness of any service-learning project (Cone and Harris, 1996; Lipka, 1997). Students had a chance to reflect on their experience of the project in classroom discussions and in sessions with a student assistant working with the Steans Center. It is through these reflections that we can evaluate our success at creating progressive democratic citizens.

The student reaction to the project was hardly uniform. Some students were interested in urban planning, whereas others took the class simply because it was required. Race, gender, and immigrant status also served to influence students' experiences of the project, although often in unpredictable ways. Some of the most negative reactions to Pilsen and the Mexican community's opposition to gentrification came from immigrant students from Eastern Europe. After the walking tour of the more immigrant sections of the neighborhood, one referred to the gentrified part as a "return to civilization." This student insisted that there was nothing for the community to complain about, saying that if they did not want to be displaced, they should just work harder and make more money. The student wrote, "This is America and you can do anything." This was the most extreme of the negative reactions.

In discussing why many students felt more comfortable in the more gentrified, cookie-cutter landscape of University Village, there was recognition that this was because it looked like the suburban landscapes already familiar to them.[5] In discussions, students were able to begin questioning why urban landscapes are being reshaped in this way.

Among the more interesting reactions to the project was an ethical dilemma that arose for one student whose father was a developer. With her new understanding of how gentrification works and the effects on the community, she started to question her father's work: buying places, fixing them up, and then selling them. The student and her father had been looking to buy in Pilsen as she began the class. They were convinced that within ten years, Pilsen would gentrify and become a high-income neighborhood like Lincoln Park. In one guided reflection, the student reported having struggled with working in the Pilsen community on behalf of the Pilsen Alliance, representing a group that wants to stop people like her father from coming into their neighborhood in search of profitable real estate development.

While not all students changed their opinions over the course of the project, they were at least more educated about the issues at play. Many started the course thinking that gentrification is inevitable. At the end of the term, many still saw gentrification as a good option, but they could at least understand why some segments of the population might be opposed. Part of the education process was students realizing a sense of ownership over the knowledge they had acquired while doing their block inventories. One student expressed being confused by the declining real estate values on her block and asked what might be causing that. In providing suggestions, we urged her to come up with her own theory, arguing that there was no one who knew more about this particular block than she did. This seemed to surprise her. Ultimately it drove her to come up with her own interpretation. Students were discussing and comparing the results of their blocks together. Their ownership of this data provided them with an actual basis for arguing their views.

Harpreet Gill, a geography student and the coauthor of this paper, has had the opportunity to follow the project from the first stage, as a student in the introductory Urban Geography course conducting the building inventory, to the community mapping process, where she entered data into a GIS program and participated in presenting the outcomes to the community. She is perhaps the best able to reflect on the totality of the project, as student, researcher, community advocate, and future urban planner.

The Urban Geography course taught students about the factors and people that shape land use in urban areas. The service-learning portion of it was an opportunity to see what kind of work goes into organizing a community to properly plan its land use.

Students have a tendency to think that land use happens naturally. If someone owns land, they should have the right to do what they want with it. If a city needs something somewhere, eventually it will get it. But it is not always the taxpayers who decide how their money should be used. The course showed that urban policy is about who has the power and voice to bring issues to the table.

The experience in the field showed students how to be active in community development. The Pilsen Alliance has a plan, and students are helping them carry it out. Now that we are using the data we collected to make visual representations of quantitative and qualitative data, it is much easier to talk about the changes occurring in the neighborhood so the community can decide what should be done about it. This will give the community an opportunity to decide where they stand and what should or should not be done. The data collection and the maps are tools for educating the community, as well as ways to connect what was being taught in the classroom to the real world issues.

Conclusions

As with any student-centered project, the problems and possibilities lie within the student body. When relying on students, we are vulnerable to those who do not take their responsibilities seriously. We have had students omit or even fabricate large chunks of data; however, we also have had students who discovered new web sites with additional information that we ended up incorporating into our data set.

The fact that this project relies more on quantitative data than personal interaction in the community is both a strength and a weakness. The data set provides us with a visible end goal that is useful to the community. But it entails some tedious data collection that left some students feeling that they have not truly connected with the community. In this way it fails in one of the fundamental goals of establishing direct experience in service-learning (Lipka, 1997). One comment that students made after completing their blocks of the community-mapping project was that they were unable to envision the extent of the project as a whole and how their contribution fits into the bigger picture. Some students did encounter community members while on their walking tours or performing their inventory, and most reported these interactions as highlights of their overall experience with the project. We should restructure the course to include a way for students to have more access to Pilsen residents, perhaps by attending community meetings.[6]

Again, the long-term nature of this project is both a strength and weakness. The continuing maintenance of the building inventory is a project that we can continue to develop. Unfortunately, the lack of immediatly visible results makes it difficult for students to see the outcomes of their work and how they have made a difference. There is a gap between their analysis and any substantive change. On the bright side, the fact that this is an issue for students means that they care enough to want to make a change and to know what happens with the story we develop over the course of the project.

In closing, CbSL is a powerful pedagogical tool for urban geography. Community work, especially around the potent political issue of gentrification, grounds many of the urban issues and developments that we discuss in the classroom. It enables us to make a substantive contribution to a community that is fighting gentrification, a struggle we deem necessary and important. Also, it is a crucial component of educating our students to become active, engaged participants in democratic progressive communities. CbSL is a process that requires a commitment and sense of responsibility from university, faculty, students, and the community and is equally reliant on all of these actors. Although the process and the project may be full of complexities and will not always meet everyone's expectations, it is a vitally important place to start to unite the university, researchers, students, and the community in enacting real change.

Acknowledgments

This project was made possible by Alex Papadopoulos, Sarah Elwood, Howard Rosing and the staff of the Steans Center for Community-based Service Learning, Alejandra Ibañez and the Pilsen Alliance, and DePaul University students.

Endnotes

1) Redlining describes a common bank policy in which red lines are literally drawn on city maps, outlining neighborhoods in which banks refuse to lend money.

2) At this juncture in mid 2004, because of the scale of the project conceived, two other institutions became involved: the University of Illinois–Chicago, whose graduate students offered to coordinate the data collection, develop a standardized building survey, and transform the material collected by DePaul University undergraduate students into a Geographic Information System; and The Resurrection Project, a Pilsen-based nonprofit organization that

builds low-income housing on land formerly belonging to the city of Chicago. Formal Institutional Review Board approval from DePaul University for expanding the project was also sought and obtained.

3) Many students reported having conversations—both positive and negative—with local residents. A majority of these students were white and middle class and, thus, to many in Pilsen, they looked like gentrifiers. Some students were verbally abused and threatened by residents.

4) As a result of meeting a member of the Pilsen Alliance during the walking tour, one of our students attained a postgraduation internship with the organization.

5) University Village is a 68-acre, 930-unit mixed-use development immediately north of Pilsen and in proximity to UIC. A second project is the 11-acre University Commons. Located on the site of the South Water Market, a former distribution and sales center for fresh produce, when completed University Commons will have 850 loft and condominium residential units (initial sales prices being $209,900 to $389,900). The developers maintain that 7% of the units will be "affordable" and priced at $210,000 for a two-bedroom apartment.

6) Expanding the project to enable students to meet with and speak to members of the community would necessitate a revised project outline to be presented to DePaul's Institutional Review Board for approval.

References

Adelman, W. J. (1983). *Pilsen and the West Side: A tour guide to ethnic neighborhoods, architecture, restaurants, wall murals, and labor history with special emphasis on events connected with the great upheaval of 1877.* Chicago, IL: Illinois Labor History Society.

Cone, D., & Harris, S. (1996, Fall). Service-learning practice: Developing a theoretical framework. *Michigan Journal of Community Service Learning, 3*, 31–43.

Cruz, W. (2004). *Puerto Rican Chicago.* Charleston, SC: Arcadia.

Curran, W. (2001). City policy and urban renewal: A case study of Fort Greene, Brooklyn. Middle States Geographer. In I. Miyares, M. Pavlovskaya, & G. Pope (Eds.), *From the Hudson to the Hamptons: Snapshots of the New York metropolitan area* (pp. 73–82). Washington, DC: Association of American Geographers.

Davis, M. (1998). *Ecology of fear: Los Angeles and the imagination of disaster.* New York, NY: Metropolitan Books.

Gans, H. J. (1962). *The urban villagers: Group and class in the life of Italian-Americans.* New York, NY: Free Press of Glencoe.

Hague, E. (2004a, May). *Connecting with Chicago's communities: Developing undergraduate research with the Pilsen Alliance.* Paper presented at the Conference on Chicago Research and Public Policy, Chicago, IL.

Hague, E. (2004b). *Gentrification and the community struggle over zoning regulations in Pilsen, Chicago.* Paper presented at the Critical Geography Mini-Conference, Terre Haute, IN.

Harvey, D. (1989). From managerialism to entrepreneurialism: The transformation in urban governance in late capitalism. *Geografiska Annaler, 71B*(1), 3–17.

Jackson, K. T. (1985). *Crabgrass frontier: The suburbanization of the United States.* New York, NY: Oxford University Press.

Jacobs, J. (1961). *The death and life of great American cities.* New York, NY: Vintage Books.

Kim, G. (2004, March 18). Pilsen residents win vote on zoning. *Chicago Tribune*, p. 3.

Lipka, R. P. (1997). Research and evaluation in service learning: What do we need to know? In J. Schine (Ed.), *Service learning: Ninety-sixth yearbook of the National Society for the Study of Education* (pp. 56–68). Chicago, IL: University of Chicago Press.

Marcuse, P. (1986). Abandonment, gentrification, and displacement: The linkages in New York City. In N. Smith & P. Williams (Eds.), *Gentrification of the city* (pp. 153–177). Boston, MA: Allen and Unwin.

McCarthy, J. (1999). Chicago: A case study of social exclusion and city regeneration. *Cities, 16*(5), 323–331.

Pilsen Alliance. (2004). *Vision, organize, empower!* Chicago, IL: Author.

Pilsen Alliance. (2005). *Gentrification phenomenon in Pilsen: East versus West.* Chicago, IL: Author.

Smith, N. (1996). *The new urban frontier: Gentrification and the Revanchist city.* London, U.K.: Routledge.

Paradoxes of Praxis: Community-Based Learning at a Community-Based University

6

Daniel Block, Mark J. Bouman

Chicago State University (CSU) is a regional, predominantly undergraduate institution serving Chicago's South Side and southern suburbs. Although CSU serves a variety of students, the typical students are African-American women, often with children, working as well as going to school. The geography program at CSU, which houses one of the few nonprofessional master's programs at the university, has had a long-standing interest in university-community partnerships through its Frederick Blum Neighborhood Assistance Center (NAC). This is an outreach center that provides research and information for local community groups. Although students have become involved with these projects on their own, efforts have recently been made to team particular courses with local community organizations. A number of issues have surfaced from this. Many students are members of the communities involved in the partnerships, thus blurring the boundaries between community and university. This also creates conflicts between the goals of broadening students' experiences versus involving them in local issues. In addition, undergraduates who belong to these communities or who have community action experience may become leaders in these projects, blurring the boundary between undergraduate and graduate students. This chapter discusses how these conflicts play out in two courses and a research project with graduate and undergraduate participants. The courses are

Introduction to Geographic Information Systems (GIS) and Neighborhood Development; the research project is part of an effort to build a multigenerational educational pipeline that focuses on neighborhood environmental concerns. Such educational experiences should benefit the learner and the community, but there may also be important benefits for the institution when care is taken in designing programs.

A Community-Based University

Place matters: As academic geographers we take that as a given. However, when we work on service-learning projects, we often have to learn the lesson all over again. Of course, the situation of the community we serve matters. We also have come to see that we need to account for the particular circumstances of our university and of our department if we want to design an experience for students that matters to them, the community served, and the institution.

CSU serves a very particular niche in the state of Illinois. The university is located on the far south side of Chicago. Its 7,000 students hail from a region closely centered to the campus. The demography of the student body is a reflection of this region: predominantly African American, more women than men, older than so-called traditional students, and likely to be working, going to school, and raising a family at the same time. CSU is well aware of this reflection, and its mission statement speaks of "educating students where academic and personal growth and promise may have been inhibited by lack of economic, social, or educational opportunity" (CSU, 2004, ¶ 1). The most popular majors tend to be occupationally oriented fields such as education, business, nursing, and criminal justice, rather than the liberal arts and sciences. CSU has graduate programs and has just begun its first doctoral program. However, the number of students in nonprofessional degree programs is small.

The geography program in which we work began as a stand-alone service department to the College of Education, with its graduate programs geared to the needs of students in social studies secondary education. Over time that role changed, in part to stave off the declining number of majors. The department began to focus on other elements in the geographers' toolkit such as GIS and neighborhood and environmental planning. Meanwhile, small universities like CSU became especially vulnerable to statewide higher education budget cuts, leading to several rounds of program consolidation. Today, geographers work in the Department of Geography, Sociology, Economics, and Anthropology.

Neighborhood and environmental planning issues in the region are perhaps stronger today than they ever have been. The Calumet area, where CSU is located, saw 20,000 manufacturing jobs lost in the 1980s. In this region, 700 hazardous substance producers continue to operate, and significant contamination is suspected at 87 sites. Environmental injustice, sustainable development, and brownfields (abandoned industrial sites with unknown environmental problems) have everyday currency here (Bouman, 2001). Geographers seemed to have the right mix of skills to help the university relate to these issues, and they certainly had the necessity of finding a niche for their discipline. A National Research Council report makes the case that "geography is useful, perhaps even necessary, in meeting certain societal needs" (Rediscovering Geography Committee, National Research Council, 1997, p. ix)

Since the early 1990s geographers at CSU have built a program based on a committed public scholarship that integrates teaching, research, and service to the greatest extent possible, given the resource circumstances of the institution and resource and opportunity constraints of its students. CSU's urban outreach program, the NAC, operates the Calumet Environmental Resource Center, which was founded in partnership with two Chicago organizations at a time when the city of Chicago was contemplating building an international airport in the area.

One of the most important projects undertaken by the Neighborhood Assistance Center was the "Communiversity" program. The program was conceived when resources became available to the NAC. It was able to hire a full-time coordinator with faculty rank, establish a set of Communiversity internships, and set up grants for faculty release time. All of this occurred within the context of the florescence of the service-learning movement in the 1990s. The program thus became a mix of student-centered learning and community outreach.

We think of the Communiversity program as directed by the community, the institution, and the students. Each project undertaken should build capacity in all three areas, although the emphasis can vary. It is community directed when the NAC and its affiliated faculty take the lead in establishing a community resource, such as the Lake Calumet Ecosystem Partnership program, and within that collaborative framework advocate for community interests (see Peterman, 2004). For example, when the city of Chicago released a draft land-use plan for the Calumet region, the fate of one patch of open space known as Van Vlissingen Prairie was not resolved. Its owner, the Norfolk Southern Railroad, wanted to expand the site for a new intermodal rail yard. Members of the partnership lent their voice to support an alternative use as a rehabilitated natural area. That is what happened, and the site is now known as the Marian Byrnes Natural Area, named for a community activist who fought for its open-space status. The student project was developed with the Chicagoland Bicycle Federation through contacts within the ecosystem partnership.

Some programs are more directed at building the capacity of the institution to expand its outreach into the community. An example is the partnership with Wilbur Wright College, one of the two-year city colleges of Chicago, to develop an environmental entrepreneurship partnership in the atmospheric sciences with a National Oceanic and Atmospheric Administration (NOAA) grant.

At other times, the emphasis is on the student learner, as in the GIS project conducted with the Southeast Environmental Task Force. The focus of the project was on teaching students in the sort of real-world context where most GIS problems are framed.

Geographic Information on the Southeast Side

Work on behalf of a local environmental organization was seamlessly integrated into the lectures and labs of Introduction to Geographic Information Systems, taught by Jason Biller.[1] GIS may be defined as the process of storing, collecting, analyzing, and presenting information for spatial decision-making purposes. It has been of great interest to community organizations, but at the same time, communities encounter barriers of access to this technology. GIS includes investments and upgrades to hardware and software, database management, and staff time to manage these issues and to interface them with the organization's goals. How to overcome these issues has been of prime concern to a sector of the GIS community, dubbed the study of Public Participation GIS (PPGIS; Craig, Harris, & Weiner, 2002). While Biller was not primarily interested in teaching his students PPGIS, the long-term relationships built between the NAC and the environmental task force enabled him to advance the goals of both organizations and his own goal of teaching students introductory GIS.

Biller was hired with the expectation that these activities would need to be relevant to the surrounding region. He attended monthly meetings of the Lake Calumet Ecosystem Partnership (facilitated by the NAC staff) and came to know the environmental task force through those meetings. The task force received a grant through the Northeastern Illinois Planning Commission to conduct a Common Ground project. For this project, community organizations assisted the planning commission in collecting field information at a finer level of detail than the commission would otherwise collect. They approached Biller and asked if this was something he could incorporate into a course.

The primary goal for the course was to have students gain an understanding of the GIS process, including learning and applying appropriate techniques in building spatial databases, doing basic analysis, and creating map layouts. What made it possible for Biller to agree to the environmental task force project was that he felt the best way to accomplish these goals would be to have students perform a GIS project for a local community group. Students would have a real-world connection to the GIS process. They would analyze the problem, determine the available data and the gaps for the particular project, collect raw data using global positioning technology, incorporate the data into a framework appropriate for analysis, and develop output. In so doing, students would also be exposed to the important role of the interrelationship between GIS analysts and clients. Finally, student output would be presented to the members of the environmental task force.

The course presumed no prior knowledge of GIS or of the Calumet region. Students were introduced to the Calumet region and the environmental task force's project goals as Biller taught GIS analysis, including the intricacies associated with the use of the software and the content of the particular research problem. The environmental task force had started the first phase of an urban planning process, called the Calumet Corridor Visioning process, to link its work in environmental restoration to potential ecotourism in the region. They sought to map four transportation corridors in the area for existing restaurants, bars, parking, traffic, and other amenities. Because CSU operates on a 16-week semester, students only had time to map two and one-half transportation corridors.

One of several modifications that needed to be made as the course progressed was the use of new research technologies. Initially, the planning commission protocol specified field data collection using hand-held personal digital assistants such as Palm Pilots. That method proved to be too slow and fraught with technical difficulties. Instead, students used global positioning technology (Trimble GeoXT) purchased for the CSU department under the NOAA grant. This technology allows one to enter geographically precise information about parcels of land into a database.

Biller also needed to pay close attention to how he worked with the students. To save class time, he did some preproject data collection so that he could anticipate any technical troubles. He carefully thought through what was feasible for actual data collection within the constraints of a 16-week course while still being able to deliver the regular course content. The actual field data collection took place over a two-week period with 14 students broken into six teams of two or three students. The teams were based on several considerations. First, data collection with a shared global positioning unit was more manageable. Second, students were matched by the times they were available for field work. Field data were collected Monday through Saturday from 8:00 a.m. to 5:30 p.m. for five to six hours at a time. This allowed everyone in a particular team to be driven from campus to the neighborhood in which they conducted research. This setup worked for all but one student who had consistent problems with being on time. Third, Biller tried to match students according to their interests: environment, recreation, and planning. Students reported that the course was overall an excellent experience, although it was cold and sometimes rainy.

Biller was extraordinarily available for this work. He drove everyone to their research sites and to the environmental task-force office, walked them through the data collection process, and introduced them to the local neighborhood culture. He even bought them lunch.

Was the class a success? In terms of teaching Introduction to GIS, it was. Students were not force-fed lecture material but learned how to solve problems in the context of a real-world setting. Biller adopted the approach the next time he taught the course. It should be noted that the work took place in the Hegewisch community area, an isolated community a few miles from campus with few African-American residents. Biller's efforts to make the students feel at home in this environment greatly contributed to their learning experience and overcame their initial anxieties.

Was the class a success in terms of working with the environmental task force? There were technical issues in outputting data and reformatting it for the purpose of creating a final project for the planning commission. Although Biller and the environmental task force are still working on that, he feels that the project strengthened the ongoing relationship between CSU and the environmental task force.

One outcome of the project is that it created a useful introductory module to the study of GIS, because it incorporated so many elements of a typical project. The most important elements included data collection in the field, the transfer of data to an integrated GIS program, and the creation and design of electronic maps. Biller presented an introduction to GIS using this case study at the Calumet Research Summit sponsored by the city of Chicago in January 2006.

A Community-Directed Project

The partnership between the NAC and the bicycle federation is an example of a community-directed project that was integrated into a class. Recently, the bicycle federation has been trying to broaden its geographic scope to advocate for bicycle-friendly roads and trails into underserved neighborhoods, mainly of color, such as Chicago's South Side and southern suburbs. As part of this advocacy, the bicycle federation hired an organizer to focus on Chicago's South Side African-American communities. They contacted the NAC through a suggestion from the director of the environmental task force. The bicycle federation was looking in particular to research a possible new bike trail running along the Calumet-Sag Channel, a canal that links the Little Calumet River, the Des Plaines River, and the Great Lakes and Mississippi shipping systems. The canal runs through communities of a variety of incomes and ethnicities and passes by a number of particularly low-income communities with few parks and other amenities. The bicycle federation asked for help in finding students who might be interested in researching the characteristics of these communities. The bicycle federation was particularly interested in CSU's status as a community university and the fact that many of its students are from the area that would be the focus of the research.

The bicycle federation hoped to find a graduate student interested in doing a thesis on the topic. Although the geography program has recently developed a thesis option, there were no students forthcoming. The project did, however, fit the course requirements for Neighborhood Development, a required course for CSU's master's program in community economic development. As is true for many classes in the geography program, the Neighborhood Development course is cross listed and therefore available to graduate and undergraduate students. In spring 2005 only four of the 16 students enrolled in the course were undergraduates, and of those only one was a so-called traditional student. Four graduate students were taking the class at a beginning level and eight at a more advanced level. This is a typical trend for cross-listed courses in the program. The mixing of graduate and undergraduate students in such CSU classes created interesting relationships within the course community. As one might expect, the graduate students often act as models and leaders; it is hoped that this pulls the undergrads and beginning graduate students further along the educational pipeline. However, the undergraduates are often nearly as knowledgeable about the world and community as the graduates and are almost as likely to become class leaders.

The project took up much of the last half of the semester. For the project, the class was divided into four teams. Each team was composed of one undergraduate student, one lower-level graduate student, and two upper-level graduate students. Teams were paired so that the most experienced students (two students who worked for city governments, for instance) were separated. The upper-level graduate students were supposed to act as team leaders. Each team was asked to turn in a report on three or four communities in the area surrounding the trail. Undergraduate students were asked to assemble a demographic census, crime statistics, and health data on each area and write a short paper describing the areas and the data. Upper-level graduate students were assigned to create asset maps of the communities describing the assets of the particular community, including the number of governmental organizations and recreational opportunities available in the community (the asset-based approach for studying communities involves focusing on community assets rather than needs). Each team was also asked to go to the communities and perform windshield surveys on the number of bicyclists and potential trail users observed in the community, along with impressions of the proposed route. Windshield surveys are performed by driving or walking through an area and collecting basic data, such as the number of buildings of various types or the number of pedestrians and bicyclists.

Prior to beginning the project, the bicycle federation organizer came to the class to help fire up interest in the project and explain the importance of the research to their goals and the region. Overall, the success of the project for the bicycle federation and the students was mixed. Despite the pleadings of the organizer and the professor to treat the assignment as a job, rather than just homework, students put varying degrees of work into the project and were at varying skill levels, particularly in writing. For example, a number of students did not finish the project or finished it very late. An undergraduate student and an advanced graduate student disappeared from the class, and a number of graduate students took incompletes. This greatly affected the work of some teams. Since the students were split into several different teams, the client still received some useful information about the communities that could be used for further research. The bicycle federation did use the report, but not extensively. The federation remained disappointed not to have attracted a graduate student to conduct a more in-depth study.

Student enjoyment and interest in the project was related to the dynamics of their research team. Some teams spent a number of days in the field, talking to village officials, community leaders, and others about the new bike trail. Others worked together very little and seemed to have generally less interest in the project. Interestingly, it was not necessarily the advanced graduate students who acted as leaders. Two undergraduate students were quite spirited and active in organizing outings to the communities. This probably comes out of the nature of the class and of CSU, where undergraduates have similar backgrounds and life experience to graduate students.

Community Air-Quality Study

In our third example, service-learning as such was not involved, although the community-service ethos informed how we set up this project. Keeping an eye on public scholarship and service-learning opportunities inherent in the department and university's position in the world ramified this project in a number of somewhat surprising directions.

The seed for the Community Air-Quality Study was a grant obtained through the NOAA to set up an environmental entrepreneur partnership in the oceanic and atmospheric sciences such as meteorology, climatology, and remote sensing.[2] The program was attractive at CSU, because it afforded an opportunity to strengthen atmospheric sciences and because air quality was such a significant issue for the city's Southeast Side. A somewhat ironic obstacle to being awarded the grant in the first place was that NOAA defined its minority audience as Historically Black Colleges and Universities or Minority-Serving Institutions. In spite of its 85% African-American enrollment, CSU did not qualify.[3] A partner needed to be found.

Wilbur Wright College (WWC), located far from CSU on the northwest side of the city of Chicago, fit the bill. WWC is one of the city colleges of Chicago and qualifies as a Minority-Serving Institution with an enrollment that is 47% Latino, 8% African American, and 7% Asian. The college offers the only environmental technology program leading to an associate's degree in the State of Illinois. Because students training in that program frequently learn by doing fieldwork at the degraded industrial sites of the Calumet region, WWC was pleased to develop more institutional linkages in the region. The two institutions turned out to be excellent partners, and they worked hard to establish a meaningful relationship even though they were 20 miles apart.

Because WWC is a two-year institution and CSU's geography program offers bachelor's and master's degrees, it was possible to think of the two schools as creating a potential environmental careers pipeline. Perhaps it would be possible to extend the pipeline in one direction to high school and middle school and in the other to a local population of adult learners. In any case, the two partners declared that they would work through the Lake Calumet Ecosystem Partnership, which was at the time facilitated by CSU through monthly meetings. They planned to work on air-quality issues on the Southeast Side of Chicago and keep an eye on opportunities to extend the pipeline during the three-year period of the grant.

Working on air quality is a matter of great local concern in a city with a high incidence of asthma and other respiratory difficulties. The Chicago region is classified as a nonattainment area for the U.S. Environmental Protection Agency's ambient air quality standards for fine particulate matter, or what the environmental literature refers to as PM 2.5. These very fine particles could be generated anywhere, although the Southeast Side, with its power plants, blast furnaces, lime kilns, and materials storage and transfer yards has a number of possible sources. The Illinois Environmental Protection Agency maintains four permanent air monitors, but these are located at the corners of the region. Given the density of possible dust sources, local community environmental activists, led by the environmental task force, believed there was an opportunity to create a finer-grained sampling network. The grant funded the purchase of a portable fine particulate air monitor for this purpose. This instrument is a portable beta attenuation monitor, or EBAM, which became the focus of a variety of outreach activities at various points in the pipeline. The grant also funded a number of student internships at both schools, and these were deployed with great flexibility in order to try to build the pipeline. Middle school students learned about the EBAM at the annual Calumet Stewardship Day in spring 2004. At this event, more than 750 children participated in a variety of environmental activities at a state park on the Southeast Side, moving through about 20 stations. Each year students from WWC and CSU spent the day manning a station that demonstrated how the EBAM worked and why it mattered. At first, this was strictly a volunteer opportunity for students from the two institutions, but later, students who were working in local internships were expected to attend.

High school students from the three schools nearby also attended Calumet Stewardship Day in its first few years. But high school student involvement in the air-monitoring project was seen in two other ways as well. Interns from CSU's geography program worked with the Calumet Is My Backyard (CIMBY) community service project operated by the Building Opportunities for Leadership Development (BOLD) Chicago Institute, a community service initiative. BOLD was founded to assist local high schools in meeting their mandatory curricular community service objectives. CIMBY led students through a series of environmental restoration and education projects in spring 2004. The CSU students worked with the high school students and taught them how to use the global positioning equipment. Once again the project incorporated graduate and undergraduate students, giving them supervisory roles. CIMBY students, who first attended a two-week HAZWOPER (hazardous waste handling operations) training at WWC, were stationed in environmental services firms for the duration of the summer.

At the core collegiate level of the partnership, the WWC and CSU programs were linked through the signing of a formal course articulation agreement that would facilitate transfer from the associate's program at WWC to the baccalaureate program at CSU. WWC developed a new Introduction to Weather course and added it to the curriculum. Faculty from both campuses made visits to each other's classrooms. Classes from both institutions took joint field trips to NOAA facilities, such as the National Weather Service forecasting office. WWC staff adopted the EBAM for a few months and calibrated it on their campus.

After this calibration and instructional period, the monitoring project was ready to begin. This involved a community-organizing effort by the environmental task force and, ultimately, the rounding up of local volunteers to put a mobile particulate monitor in their backyard. The network became the focus of work for several CSU students, through an urban planning class, an independent research course, and internships with the environmental task force. The project also became the cornerstone of one student's master's thesis. The student, Heidi Howerton, began as staff at WWC, moved to take the HAZWOPER course, enrolled at CSU, and in the end served as the point person on the partnership. Howerton embodied the goals of the partnership to move underrepresented people into the atmospheric sciences while studying an issue of local concern.

From April through October 2005, monitor readings were obtained at two-week intervals from the backyards of a dozen volunteers. Community residents contributed to the project not only by lending their backyards but also by filling out logbooks of unusual environmental occurrences in the region, such as unusual nighttime plant operations. Moving the monitor from one site to another and calibrating it at the new location was an arduous and time-consuming process accomplished by several CSU students.

During the summer of 2005, 20 high school students from CSU's PREMAT precollege science preparatory experience (administered through the Department of Chemistry and Physics) center their summer's investigations around preliminary data from the EBAM. They correlated particulate readings from the instrument with daily weather observations. They presented their work to members of the Southeast Side community, who came to CSU for students' presentations.

Was this project successful as a service-learning initiative? Most of the college students involved joined the project through internships, independent studies, or thesis courses. But as we discussed above, the service-learning ethos pervaded the project and ultimately built a number of bridges that are likely to lead to more traditional service-learning opportunities in the future.

Conclusions

A number of issues arise from the practice of community-university partnerships in general and the particular situation of CSU. First, there is a blurring of the community-university divide when many of the students are members of the community involved in the partnership. Second, there is a blurring of the boundaries between undergraduate and graduate students. Third, there are conflicts between the goals of broadening students' experiences versus involving them in local issues. Logistically, community-based projects can be very difficult, given the time constraints of nontraditional students. The financial constraints of such students also need to be taken into account when assessing the successes and failures of student-centered learning. Almost all CSU students work, often to provide for their families, and most classes are at night. Group projects during the day might mean taking time off from work. In such a circumstance, instructors need to be particularly careful that service-learning does not become nothing more than unpaid work for a community organization—it should have particular relevance to the students' training and understanding of the world.

In practice the research opportunities described here generally took place in more professionally oriented classes within the geography department that were first and foremost training exercises. However, the most successful students' ultimate experience was that they received more than only field training. They were exposed to communities they did not know well and learned more about the community they live in. Even at a university where most students have had ample life experiences, knowledge of their own and surrounding communities tends to be weak. The research opportunities allowed students to discover and hopefully appreciate their surroundings in new and more nuanced ways.

The blurring of the undergraduate-graduate divide at CSU generally aids the undergraduate research experience. Although traditional full-time graduate students are hard to find, undergraduates are generally treated as equals in cross-listed courses. Students most often do not know who is a graduate student and who is an undergraduate. The circumstances of the course mean that undergraduates are allowed to be leaders. In the bicycle federation study, for instance, graduate students were asked to lead and do more work. In at least two teams, undergraduates were just as active in leading and organizing the research. This blurring was also true in the NOAA project where undergraduates, graduate students, and two-year students worked with community members to gather data. In a best-case scenario, this blurring would not only help interested students progress up the educational pipeline, but it would also keep more advanced students focused by bringing in undergraduates with their own sets of skills and interests.

There are definitely barriers to doing the community-based research we have described at a community university. Many area groups have few resources. To them a university is a large organization with many resources that should be channeled directly back to the community. Although this is part of the purpose of the NAC, on the university side the reality is that there is little money available for community assistance. It would have been great, for instance, to be able to provide an intern for the bicycle federation, but CSU students almost always need paid internships. At the moment there is no money at CSU to provide for such positions. The particular projects that are undertaken should also match the course goals. This was truer in the GIS course than the Neighborhood Development course, and the more successful outcome of the project for the client followed from this. Placing a project in a class just to serve a community organization helps nobody. Finally, the university may be asked to do research that might help only certain stakeholders. In a recent case, the NAC was asked to do research on transportation problems that might result from the opening of a new nearby mega-church, to which many CSU students belong. As we are part of the community and a state university, the issue was deemed simply too sensitive for us to provide more than minimal data. It would have been particularly unwise to require a class to conduct this type of research. A student might have been placed in a position where she or he would be required to do research that could have an adverse effect on the expansion of their own church. Despite these barriers, community-based, student-performed research is extremely important to CSU, both in fulfilling its mission as a community-based university and in training students to be informed citizens. Such research also creates a forum for interaction between students of different levels and may help promote the formation of pipelines of students from level to level.

Endnotes

1) Jason Biller is the administrator of the CSU GIS laboratory and also teaches one course per term in the GIS sequence. We thank him for sharing details of his course with us.

2) Award #NA16AE2932. Victoria Cooper of WWC is the director of the environmental technology program and was the principal investigator on the NOAA grant, and Mark Bouman was the co-principal investigator.

3) CSU began in the immediate post-Civil War period as the Cook County Normal School and for much of the 20th century was known as Chicago Teachers' College. African-American students became the majority in the 1970s.

References

Bouman, M. J. (2001). Ten keys to the landscape of the Calumet Region. *Journal of Geography, 100*(3), 104–110.

Chicago State University. (2004). *Mission statement.* Retrieved September 27, 2006, from: http://www.csu.edu/strategicplanning resources/missionstatement.htm

Craig, W. J., Harris, T. M., & Weiner, D. (Eds.). (2002). *Community participation and geographical information systems.* New York, NY: Taylor and Francis.

Peterman, W. (2004). Advocacy vs. collaboration: Comparing inclusionary community planning models. *Community Development Journal, 39*(3), 266–276.

Rediscovering Geography Committee, National Research Council. (1997). *Rediscovering geography: New relevance for science and society.* Washington, DC: National Academies Press.

Action Research in a Visual Anthropology Class: Lessons, Frustrations, and Achievements

7

S. Elizabeth Bird, Jess Paul Ambiee, James Kuzin

Is it possible to complete a meaningful piece of community action research with a small team of students within the confines of a one-semester course? This question worried me for most of the Fall 2004 semester. Toward the end of the following semester, as the concrete outcomes could be assessed, I believed the answer was generally positive, even though we had set ourselves rather lofty goals—technologically, practically, and ethically.[1]

The class was Visual Anthropology, a subject that does not immediately suggest community action research. Visual anthropology has long focused on the making of ethnographic film, analysis of visual images, and the consideration of practical and ethical concerns involved in their use and dissemination. More recently, there has been a growing concern with indigenous media and a move toward people representing themselves rather than being represented by anthropologists. Even more recently, some visual anthropologists have begun to develop applied visual anthropology. This uses visual anthropological theory, methodology, and practice to achieve applied or so-called nonacademic ends, including helping to facilitate social interventions and problem solving. The developing field of applied visual anthropology includes indigenous or participatory media and techniques, such as photo elicitation. This requires working with people to visually represent their culture in order to help bring about social change in places such as schools and health care settings (Pink, 2004).

The class, which met once a week, spent the first few weeks reading, critiquing, and becoming familiar with the key ideas in visual anthropology and brainstorming about the applied research project. In the past, I had allowed students to pick topics and work individually, without an applied requirement. This time I wanted to situate the projects more firmly within the University of South Florida (USF) Department of Anthropology's explicit commitment to applied anthropology. I also wanted to explore the possibilities of genuinely engaged research such as drawing on models developed by other social scientists (Holland, 1997; McTaggart, 1997; Ramaley, 2001). My goal was to find a project in which students would not merely volunteer in the community but would observe and reflect upon their work and explicitly connect theory with practice. Furthermore, I wanted to involve a community partner both in the development of the research questions and in the creation of results that would benefit the partner. I wanted to ensure that students gained experience of team ethnography—the setting in which most practicing anthropologists find themselves.

The Community Partner: Prodigy

We found our partner in the Prodigy Cultural Arts Program, located close to the university. It is one of many social and educational services offered through the University Area Community Center, a state-of-the art facility dedicated in June 2002, built on land once used as a homeless camp and illegal dump. The program provides cultural arts programming for prevention, intervention, and diversion and is expected annually to serve 336 diversion youth adjudicated through the Hillsborough County court system for nonviolent first offenses. The program serves 500 intervention youth considered at risk, because they have parents or siblings in the corrections system, and an additional 1,000 siblings, family, and community youth. Also, children from outside the area are served by the program, which is funded through the Office of Juvenile Justice and Delinquency Prevention and managed through the School of Social

Work at USF, with further assistance from Hillsborough Community College and McGill University in Canada. Thus the concept of a university partnership was familiar and valued.

Prodigy's mission is to positively affect juvenile antisocial behavior through the visual and performing arts, including music, dance, theater, and comedy. It offers opportunities for self-expression and skills that allow children to work with each other across ethnic lines. It also offers opportunities to learn discipline in the arts, which could apply to other parts of their lives. A key figure in its development was Florida State Senator Victor Crist, chairman of the University Area Community Development Corporation (UACDC). He helped initiate the program in part to quantitatively test the plethora of anecdotal evidence on the success of the mission statement. To provide data the USF School of Social Work is undertaking a systematic evaluation of Prodigy outcomes, building on the existing literature of the social impact of arts programs. In its own literature, Prodigy claims such successes as higher school attendance rates, improved grades, decreased disciplinary referrals, and drastically lowered crime rates. It states 98% of participants are crime free—figures that are said to be 46% higher than the national rates for such intervention programs.

Current Prodigy Director Carolena von Trapp began her tenure in 2004. Since its inception in 2000, the program had been plagued by low youth enrolment, high staff turnover, and what von Trapp perceived as lack of overall direction. With a background in anthropology, community arts programming, and business, she was brought in to expand the program's vision. She defined it as emphasizing the positive embrace of cultural heritage and ethnic diversity, and the realization of agency in the students fostered through their coconstruction of knowledge in the classroom with a child-centered program. It also promotes recognition of social responsibility through the following of mutually agreed-upon rules of conduct and collaborative learning methods. It emphasizes encouragement of imagination and creativity, with a focus on social purpose, which allows students to see the broader implications of events in their lives. She sees the program as an alternative to the structured, knowledge-based curricula of formal schools. Von Trapp hired several new arts instructors, most of them performers with some teaching experience, rather than teachers trained for public education. She has worked on developing a bottom-up approach with a collaborative sense of purpose. She holds a master's degree in applied anthropology and is enrolled in the USF doctoral program. This creates an unusually good fit between our goals and hers, and she saw our research team as another collaborator in her transformative mission.

The Prodigy Neighborhood

The geographic area served by the Prodigy program is north of Tampa, near USF. Known officially as the University Area, it is also commonly called Suitcase City because of high levels of transient occupancy. It began as student housing for USF, but as the university grew, students moved away and the area's vacancy rate grew. The apartment complexes were largely owned by absentee landlords, and the area went through a spiral of decline as properties were bought, sold, or repossessed. When maintenance was no longer cost effective, buildings were left to rot, and rents settled at rates that are among the lowest in the county, following an influx of lower income populations.

The area began to experience the hardships of larger urban centers. It became one of the most densely populated areas in Florida with unemployment double the median rate and the highest concentration of teenage pregnancy, single mothers, infant mortality, illiteracy, public assistance users, and building code violations in the greater Tampa Bay region. Aggravated assaults, rapes, robberies, and drug-related crimes greatly exceeded the county averages. Ninety percent of the children received free lunch, and three out of four moved every year. Although the area had only 3% of the juveniles in the county, it accounted for 10% of juvenile offenses and lacked social and cultural resources. A lack of a park, library, or school in the area left few options for youth. Poor public transportation and lighting created unsafe conditions and cover for crime, and the neighborhood developed a highly negative public image in the 1980s and 1990s.

In 1990 community and business organizations and citizens formed the University Area Civic Association and partnered with Hillsborough

County, the U.S. Attorney's office, the Sheriff's office, and the U.S. Department of Justice to procure one of the first of only 15 Weed and Seed grants that were awarded by the Clinton administration. With this money, and through alliances forged with USF, Hillsborough Community College, Hillsborough County schools, Senator Crist, private donors, and local human services providers, the University Area Civic Association and the UACDC created an action plan to redevelop the area.

Since then the area has seen many improvements, including a new Sheriff's office, new streetlights, new sidewalks, a 28-acre community park, a community center, a magnet elementary school, and a vocational high school, and more changes are planned. In some respects, Suitcase City has emerged in 2005 as a poster child for cooperative community investment, and it was within this context that the anthropology students began their project.

Project Goals and Methodology

Prodigy has been the only U.S. participant in a five-year study, the National Youth in Arts Demonstration Project, led by researchers at McGill University. The McGill research has shown that art programs following specific protocols yield measurable outcomes. The study is continuing under the auspices of the USF School of Social Work. Our project was not intended to replicate this long-term research study but was planned to offer research training to students while producing results that would be useful to our partner.

In keeping with the goals of participatory action research (PAR), we developed our specific goals, methods, and anticipated deliverables in consultation with von Trapp. Given the focus of the class, we wanted to use visual documentation that would be useful to our partners and function as a valid research project for our students. As teacher and project leader, I also had important pedagogical goals. I wanted to ensure that lessons learned in class, such as the practical and ethical issues of visual and verbal representation, the significance of editing decisions, and the potentially different goals of client and ethnographer, would play out in a group setting. I also wanted students to experience these lessons in a real way and for them to learn the satisfaction of carrying out research that makes a difference. As McTaggart (1997) writes, action researchers "change themselves, support others in their own efforts to change, and together work to change institutions and society" (p. 34). Lofty goals indeed—but even in a small way, I hoped that the students would experience a sense of this through their involvement in the project. I began preliminary discussions with von Trapp, the class members toured the facility and met with staff and students, and a set of research goals and deliverables was developed.

It was agreed that adjudicated youth would be excluded, except peripherally, in the class project. This was decided due to the dangers of overstudying them and the ethical considerations in visual representation. Instead, the class members would observe and interview younger children, predominantly 7 to 12 years old, in after-school visual arts and music classes, with some attention given to classes in drama, dance, and comedy arts. We agreed that the ethnographic study would take place over a five-week period, because classes were run on five-week cycles, meeting for about 90 minutes twice a week. Interviews and informal interaction were taped for a video project, and students spent considerable time observing and interacting with teachers and children without cameras present. They frequently acted as volunteer classroom assistants and honed their skills as participant-observers and interviewers, because several had no experience in practical ethnography. We worked with the program to create release forms for children who would appear on camera and did not interview children whose parents had not consented.

The project was not conceived as a program evaluation or an attempt to measure social gains. Many claims have been made about the positive impact of community arts programs, from social benefits to public health gains, although definitive documentation is elusive. Indeed, Newman, Curtis, and Stephens (2003) point to the difficulty of quantifying social gains, suggesting that many studies "failed to meet the most demanding methodological criteria" (p. 313). Moriarty (1997) argues that the benefits of arts programs are often intangible and difficult to see and indeed may not be apparent until later in life. Our goal here was to complement the quantitative study with an attempt to elicit the point of view of teachers and children. Von Trapp believed such a perspective would be useful to her work on cultural change, and she welcomed the possibilities of the students' findings. The guiding issues included the apparent meaning of Prodigy to children and teachers, whether Prodigy was going beyond artistic skills to achieve learning with a social purpose, and whether teachers believed the goals of creating a child-centered program were being achieved. Also important was what we could observe about the nature of interactions among children and between children and teachers, and whether there seemed to be a shared vision with Prodigy.

We hoped to be able to understand some of the more intangible achievements of Prodigy and to document these to our partners. In consultation with von Trapp, we planned to produce several deliverables: a report of our ethnographic work, a set of high-quality digital photos that could also be used by the program, and a short video that captured the spirit of Prodigy, which could be used by the program in recruiting, fundraising, and for many other purposes.

The eight students (six of whom were graduate students) in the research team formed themselves into two groups. Three planned to focus on the video, four planned to work closely in a visual arts class, and one planned to move between both groups. Six students were anthropology majors (one a mass communications double major), and they were joined by one each from the women's studies and communications departments. The visual arts group, in consultation with von Trapp, structured and created the five-week arts unit and developed a class that would allow children to document their own lives through photography. They were inspired by the visual anthropologists we had studied. This plan had to be drastically modified when it became apparent that the class teacher was not prepared to allow such an arrangement. This was an early lesson in how the community partner's wishes are not necessarily represented through one individual at the top. Instead, the visual arts group began with a more traditional participant-observation approach during the five-week research period that followed the initial consultations. They observed and interacted with children as they followed the teacher's lesson plan. They functioned as unofficial classroom assistants and prepared the children for on-camera interviews, which they conducted. At the end of the semester, we had a rough cut of the video, individual research reports, and photos, and I believe the students had a genuine sense of achievement. They also had learned crucial lessons about the perils and rewards of visual anthropology, team research, and work with a community partner.

Lessons Learned

The project gave us all new insights into the nature of the PAR approach to applied ethnography. These are lessons that I hope to apply as I plan a primarily undergraduate version of the course and that the graduate students should be able to take with them into their individual research projects. Erickson and Stull (1998) offer cautionary words about any kind of team ethnography. Many of our conclusions echo their discussion, although we believe there are other issues that are particularly important to consider when setting up team ethnography as a class experience. For instance, Erickson and Stull point out that applied anthropology must move past the Lone Ranger model of single anthropologists working in communities that are defined as "theirs." This is even more relevant when working with a community partner. This is also relevant in a class setting, where many students have internalized a competitive model of education in which they compete against each other for grades and achievement. It can be difficult for them to develop a new way of seeing—that to succeed in this venture they must work together with a common goal in mind and strive for active participation from the partner.

The Problem of Community Participation

In our project we took steps to develop that common vision. First, we developed the project concept together from several options that were raised and discussed by the project leader and the students. As advised by Erickson and Stull, we planned and maintained a regular schedule of debriefings after weekly class meetings, supplemented by frequent email communication among team members and the faculty leader. And as described above, we tried to develop our research agenda in consultation with our partners. After initial discussions, the students and Prodigy staff met informally at a mixer hosted at the community center in early October 2004, complete with wine and cheese, musical performances, and presentations of children's visual art. Students interacted with Prodigy instructors, community center administration, and Senator Crist. Members of the film team captured some of our earliest footage and conducted an interview with Crist—altogether an optimistic start to our project. At that point, the team felt the project was going to be easy sailing.

However, we soon came face to face with one of the real problems of short, class-based projects. PAR takes time, not only to complete but also to set up, and it cannot be rushed without risking the fragile relationship between partners. Flushed by success, the video team followed up the mixer by attending their first Prodigy staff meeting, with video cameras in hand, as previously approved by von Trapp. James Kuzin reported on the event: "Throughout the meeting I observed a discomfort in Carolena, who appeared to be second guessing her choice of words and phrases while making repeated reference to our camera's presence." Jess Ambiee reported in his field notes on the same event:

One of the teachers looked directly at the camera to state what he does, instead of at the director and the other staff. The director looked frustrated at me. Then a teacher stated, "Are we shooting? Hold on, let me get my posture right." This "presentation of self" by the Prodigy staff was playing a significant role in the activities we were observing and capturing on tape. At the time, this seemed like a huge methodological issue for our future visual research. We did not want to manipulate the dynamics of the events we were filming. How were we going to turn this seemingly negative methodological issue into a positive or beneficial act?

The team members learned later that the tension observed in that meeting was not only, or even primarily, a consequence of their presence, but was also connected with some issues that were simmering among the staff and were later resolved. However, the moment was important in that it made the members far more reflective about the impact of their presence, demeanor, and actions, and brought them to a more mature realization that they were essentially intruding into an existing group dynamic toward which they had to be sensitive. Kuzin met with von Trapp, who expressed her concern about the intrusiveness of the cameras and their effects on the staff. He wrote, "This feedback prompted an extensive debate over issues of methodology in the weeks to follow."

Adelman (1997) writes about the "problem of participation" in action research. Even in long-term, well-funded projects that are set up carefully over a significant period of time, securing genuine commitment and partnership is, to say the least, challenging. Austin (2003) reports on a major anthropological project that involved significant funding, complex teams of interdisciplinary academic researchers, and significant commitment from active community partners over a two-year period. In many respects, it is a model for participatory anthropological research and intervention. Even so, Austin reports that maintaining active participation was a constant struggle that involved negotiation and a balance of leadership and horizontal collaboration.

I think we all agreed from the outset that short-term, class-based projects cannot meet the most exacting standards of true partner participation, especially if they are one-time-only efforts. There simply is not enough time to develop close and active participation with all the relevant stakeholders—in this case, administration, teachers, and students. We had made an effort to get to know the teachers with whom we would be working, but we had made the mistake of substituting von Trapp's commitment for whole-hearted support from her staff. We encountered this first when our expectations of being able to direct a class were dashed. It became clear that the teacher had not been fully consulted or encouraged to make this possible. Later, when faced with the reality of an alien camera in a staff "family" meeting, even von Trapp found the experience unnerving. We feared we had irreversibly damaged rapport.

We realized some rethinking was in order. The team saw that we had been moving too fast and essentially abandoned the use of the cameras for a while. We also realized that the split between the videographers and the classroom participant-observers was not effective. We needed a more flexible, fluid arrangement so that teachers and students became comfortable with all the team members. And finally, we concluded that we needed some stronger background research so that we would all better understand the context in which we were working. This would be a task some team members needed to take on. Soon after this, one student dropped out of the degree program for personal reasons, and the seven remaining students started to reconfigure. The three remaining students of the visual arts team, Charity Kiser, Sara Dykins Callahan, and Jody Owens, continued to attend the class regularly, developing strong relationships with the children and the teacher. Kiser took on the task of assembling background research about the university neighborhood, including history and crime statistics; conducting personal interviews with two administrators of the Community Center; and learning helpful information about the larger context of the Prodigy program. Kiser and Callahan went on to play crucial roles interviewing children on camera, using their warm relationships to elicit genuine, unselfconscious responses. The visual arts teacher agreed to an on-camera interview with Callahan, having previously declined one with Kuzin, with whom she was less comfortable at the time. Meanwhile, videographer Mike Meyer roamed the classes with his camera, making a special effort to explain what he was doing to the children, allowing them to look at playbacks, and sharing the viewfinder with them.

Meanwhile, Jess Ambiee temporarily abandoned cameras and focused on developing a close rapport with music teachers and their students, observing, assisting, and preparing for later on-camera interviews. He succeeded in increasing their interest and sense of shared purpose in the video, and they enthusiastically participated in on-camera interviews. Bob Pomeroy, an experienced semiprofessional photographer, decided to focus entirely on creating a still-photo archive, and many of these images were also incorporated into the video. Pomeroy also conducted a content analysis of newspaper coverage of the area and the center. This added an interesting dimension in that students realized that media coverage had directly framed and shaped the people's own understanding of their neighborhood as crime and drug ridden. Finally, Kuzin developed what turned out to be an important role, moving among all the team activities and between the team and the Prodigy staff. He had experience with action research and community-based ethnography, whereas several other team members had little or no ethnographic experience and expressed great anxiety about it. Kuzin hosted a dinner at his home for the visual arts group in which he shared personal experiences. He also met regularly with various team members. His liaison role extended beyond the class as he developed a relationship with von Trapp in which the two talked regularly, negotiated tensions between the student team and staff, and provided regular feedback to the students from the director.

This all contributed to a sense of comfort that greatly enhanced the level of commitment from our partners. While the project never achieved the level of truly involved participation to which PAR aspires, the work that the students did created a real sense of working with our partners rather than on them. The lesson left with me was that no matter how urgent it may seem to get down to work in the class project, it is crucial to spend time laying groundwork and truly listening to the needs of the partner. This communication between instructor and partner can get underway well before the class begins, but this must be supplemented by active collaborative and rapport-building work done by students with the relevant stakeholders. Students must be prepared for the work involved in building these relationships. They must see this as an integral component of the learning experience and not as an annoyance to be dealt with as quickly as possible.

Internal Team Building

Margaret Mead (as cited in Erickson & Stull, 1998) once warned that "field teams are successful to the extent that the skills and capacities, temperaments and interests of the team members are complementary, asymmetrical, and noncompetitive" (p. 18). We learned the importance of those words early. For instance, although there was great interest in creating a video documentary, it would have failed if we had not had a team member (Meyer) who already had significant experience shooting and editing digital video. We were even more fortunate that he had an engaging and noncompetitive personality, sharing his knowledge with others who wanted to become more technologically proficient. But an action research class is not the place for students to embark on a steep technological learning curve. We learned to respect and appreciate his expertise, and he gradually learned to respect other students' proficiency in conceptualizing the story, planning, and carrying out the interviews that he filmed and edited.

Similarly, the still photography archive took on prominence in large part because of the skills of Pomeroy. Although other students also took photos, his were more professional and appropriate for use by our partners. Ambiee, Callahan, Kiser, and Owens demonstrated interpersonal skills that made them keen observers and excellent interviewers. Ambiee also spent considerable time learning video-editing skills and polishing the video script. And as discussed earlier, Kuzin's experience and personality were valuable in creating the liaison role that worked to reduce tension between team and partner as well as among team members. Although I had not explicitly planned for such a role, I anticipate building it into future projects. Kuzin's self-created task of constant debriefing—taking the lead in email discussions of issues from development of interview questions to feelings of guilt about leaving the field—was valuable. I believe the team was fortunate in that they were willing to be flexible, to move outside their comfort zone, and to support each other's strengths.

Nevertheless, fieldwork is stressful, especially in a group setting, and tensions did arise. Some emerged around the very issues I had expected to see coming out of the debates we had in classes. We had studied various models of ethnographic filmmaking, from traditional documentary to observational cinema, cinema verité, and participatory filmmaking in which the film's subjects cocreate the product. Furthermore, we had explored at great length the impact of editing and the ethical issues associated with visual representation. From the beginning, there were philosophical differences among the team members about how to create the video. These began during filming but became most significant during the editing. Meyer had previously created many video pieces that seemed closely modeled on news-style documentary, with prominent narration and short, heavily edited sound bytes. He was comfortable with the journalistic model of telling the story in which the reporter essentially decides what that story is. Other team members were more interested in whether the video would genuinely represent the worldview of Prodigy. Some advocated an observational style, trying to capture natural events and using minimal structure and narration. They were acutely aware of the possible distortions of editing long comments into short sound bytes or of matching words and images inappropriately.

Furthermore, team members had very different views of the role of the community partner. The journalistic model eschews active input of film subjects, whereas PAR and applied anthropology advocate for it. There was a great deal of agonizing about whether partner input would result in a mere public-relations product. This kind of tension is typical of community-based filmmaking. Baena, Camas, Sotelo, and Mateos (2004) describe the impasses and difficulties they encountered as professional filmmakers working with community members to make documentaries that "represent the culture and experience of a particular people in a particular space and time" (p. 144) but are also "a social intervention, and a critical commentary on aspects of our society" (p. 144). They argue that such work "is produced out of a democratic and collaborative teamwork process . . . that is as much about the team and their work together as it is about the topic of the documentary itself" (p. 144). Although some of the issues were specific to the visual focus of the project, they were all relevant to the tensions inherent in PAR: What is the balance between doing objective anthropological research and being a conduit for the agenda of the community partner? How feasible is it to offer honest critique of the partner's practices, when such critique is warranted, given the rapport and friendship for which the team has striven? Indeed, our team found the creation of the final reports and video to be an act of constant negotiation. There were times when tensions grew very high, and the role of the faculty leader became critical in providing direction.

The Team Leader Role

There are several models for team ethnography, ranging from horizontal and egalitarian to more directive, with a clear team leader. From the Prodigy experience, I would conclude that in any class-based project, the instructor must take a strong role if anything meaningful is to be achieved. As the faculty leader, I found I was constantly worrying about being heavy handed in giving direction while also becoming increasingly anxious about periods when little progress was being made because of the team's lack of agreement. I spent a great deal of time composing emails to the entire group or to some members—for instance, suggesting a draft of an interview protocol for others to modify and drafting an initial editing script when dissension about the video style threatened to stall the project. The lesson I took from this was that a class based on PAR concepts is uniquely consuming—mentally, emotionally, and simply in time. There were moments when I had to make decisions about issues, often very minor, on which there was disagreement. For instance, during final editing, Meyer wished to cut down a one-minute sequence in which a child described in great detail the process for making a pottery bowl. Meyer's journalistic sensibilities were offended by what seemed the inordinate length of the clip. Other team members and I felt it conveyed a uniquely rich ethnographic sense of the child's involvement and excitement. The clip remained uncut.

The faculty role becomes very important as the project winds down, and inevitably it becomes clear that a final, polished product will not emerge from the single semester's work. As Erickson and Stull (1998) discuss, the team leader's job is almost always to "mold the data collected by the rest of the team . . . into an integrated, coherent narrative" (p. 49). This is doubly true in a class setting. At the end of the semester, when the papers were graded and the class over, there remained much to be done: Draft the final report to the partner, chivy the students into completing the video even as they are moving on to other obligations, and insist on a run-through of presentations for the Society for Applied Anthropology. A PAR class is difficult to simply leave behind—indeed, if one did so, it would be a betrayal of the very principles of PAR. I was glad that as a tenured full professor, I did not have to worry about whether the time spent on this project would adversely affect my promotion prospects. But this is surely something more junior faculty should weigh before committing to such a project.

Outcomes

To answer our initial question: Yes, we believe that even a one-semester class project can produce tangible benefits for all stakeholders—faculty, students, and community partners. In keeping with the goals of PAR, these projects can be long term and ongoing.

Students

PAR is indeed research and not merely service. The students were able to apply the theories of visual anthropology directly in their research, making real the issues faced in their readings and discussions. Each student produced a final paper in addition to their shared work on the video. As faculty leader, I developed our work into a 40-page report that offered conclusions about the nature of the Prodigy program and offered recommendations for change. For instance, we concluded that Prodigy works effectively and has a unified sense of purpose and observable successes, based on our ethnographic observations and interviews with teachers and students. We also concluded that creating the "child-centered classroom" is an art in itself. The report showed concrete examples of the delicacy of the balance between allowing creativity to flourish and providing the structure and discipline that many children in the program need. The words of the children and teachers were woven through the report, providing powerful testimony about what we called the "Prodigy difference" and offering tangible evidence of its nonquantifiable strengths. In this respect, the students' work contributed effectively and professionally to the literature on community arts programs, offering them a great sense of achievement. Several students participated in a research presentation session at the Society for Applied Anthropology, in which we were also joined by Prodigy Director von Trapp, who reflected on the process of the research.

In addition, students had the reward of seeing their work make a tangible difference. For instance, Ambiee reported that the very process of interviewing seemed to offer the Prodigy teachers a valuable opportunity to reflect:

When I asked the teachers what their goals were, they had to think critically about them and the broader role of Prodigy. While we often tend to assume the anthropologist may have a negative impact in the field, I think our presence and our questions in themselves may have had a positive effect, encouraging the participants to be more reflective. We turned a methodological issue for us into a positive and beneficial act that actually affected how they present themselves in class. I visited Keith (a music instructor) the first day of the next five-week drumming session after our research was complete, a session with entirely new children. Keith stated the goals of the class and his teaching philosophy. His message came through very clearly, using almost the same sentences he had articulated during the taped interview. During the previous five-week session that I observed, he was never so direct with his students about his agenda.

Similarly, James Kuzin, in his liaison role, may have been able to help our partners work through a communication problem. In rethinking the philosophy of Prodigy, von Trapp had stressed how different her child-centered approach was from that used in public schools. Most of the teachers she hired were not public school arts teachers. However, some were hired before her tenure. In particular, she viewed one long-time teacher as inflexible and in some ways obstructive to her goals. The teacher in turn viewed her with some suspicion. Kuzin interviewed the teacher and concluded that in reality her philosophy was very compatible with von Trapp's, a point he diplomatically made to the director. The result was that von Trapp and the teacher met over lunch, had their first truly open discussion, and reached an understanding. Episodes like these were greatly rewarding to the students, who realized the relevance of their work in actually creating cultural change—one of the key elements of PAR (McTaggart, 1997).

For some students, the project seemed to be a genuinely transforming moment. Sara Dykins Callahan, a communications student with no field experience, began the class anxious about ethnography, and very appropriately concerned about the impact on children of developing relationships with the student team and then departing. She turned out to be a natural ethnographer, interacting warmly with children and making art with them. During the final class at Prodigy, she brought artwork for the children, sharing and saying goodbye. She made a particular study and critique of one of the class social-purpose projects and returned to Prodigy first as a volunteer and now as a paid worker. Finally, almost the entire research team came back together at the end of the following semester to present our findings and show the video to the Prodigy staff, administrators at the University Area Community Center, and Senator Crist. Again, this was a very validating experience for the faculty and students, as well as an opportunity for us to discuss the future of Prodigy with our partners.

Community Partner

As should be already clear, the benefits for the partner and the students are closely entwined, as they should be in such research. The students were rewarded through achievement that not only developed their competence as researchers, but also directly impacted our partners. At the Society for Applied Anthropology, von Trapp expressed her delight at the rich ethnographic data presented by the team report, which validated and highlighted the challenges of the cultural transformations she was trying to effect in the program. She reports that many of the team's recommendations are being implemented and had the support of the staff.

The video, a 15-minute production featuring interviews, observational footage, and the music of the Prodigy teachers and children was received enthusiastically by our community partners. It is now being used in their promotional and fundraising activities. Multiple DVD copies were made for the staff, students, and local politicians. CDs of Pomeroy's photos were also given to the program, and we have learned that they are being used extensively in their publicity and on their web page.

An especially pleasing outcome, which should herald continued collaboration, was von Trapp's decision to hire James Kuzin as a full-time assistant. As noted above, Sara Dykins Callahan also now works at Prodigy, and von Trapp has hired additional anthropology students for paid positions. Perhaps one of the greatest challenges of class-based PAR is that the work and the partnership should ideally continue beyond the research period. We see this ongoing relationship as being one of the most heartening aspects of the Prodigy project.

Faculty

I came out of this project with a strong sense of PAR as a genuine research enterprise and a significant enrichment of pedagogy. Immediate plans include a coauthored research article with von Trapp, in which we will explore the impact of the Prodigy program itself and the process of collaborative community/university anthropological research. Although I had initially conceived this project as primarily a teaching exercise, I am delighted with the way it developed into a significant piece of research in its own right. This was helped, I believe, by the fact that I spent a great deal of time at Prodigy myself, working with the students and conducting one of the on-camera interviews. For me, it was a uniquely rich and rewarding teaching experience, which I hope to repeat (although probably not every semester!).

Conclusions

In conclusion, we offer some practical suggestions that follow naturally from our work and that we believe are especially relevant to teaching a PAR class at the undergraduate level:

- Keep the class small, or at least keep groups manageable. Our group of seven worked, but it risked becoming unwieldy. In our experience, group work at the undergraduate level is especially problematic, because there is always the risk of one or more students freeloading on more committed colleagues.

- Build in mandatory debriefings, discussions, and maintenance of communication and self-reflection among group members, the faculty leader, and the community partners, who should be kept in the loop at all times. PAR is never a static approach but rather one that goes through interrelated cycles of research, reflection, and writing, much as ethnography traditionally does. As far as possible, the class should try to follow this kind of protocol, which is of course time consuming and often exhausting.

- Because of the difficulties of group work, it may be tempting to set up the class with students working on individual projects, but this should be avoided. An important dimension—the negotiation of collaborative team dynamics—would be lost, and the spirit of participatory action compromised. The group context and process are hard, but worth the effort.

- It helps to set up the community partnership in advance, but still allow time early in the semester for students to participate in the development of the research agenda. Students should feel that this is their research and not simply a task set for them.

- The message to students must be unequivocal: The class involves research, not mere community service, and there are desired research outcomes, which should be clear. Ideally, students should have prior training in research methods. If not, keep the research approach simple. As discussed in this chapter, the class is not the best place to learn how to construct a survey, carry out complex analysis, or develop sophisticated technological skills. Prescreening of students could be valuable to ensure genuine commitment and to avoid students who are simply looking for a class in a convenient time slot.

- Learn the skills, expertise, and interests of the students, and make use of them.

- The faculty leader must be an active, hands-on member of the team(s)—visible in the research and providing ongoing guidance at all times.

- She or he must be prepared to mediate disputes, offer tips for problem solving, and take an active role in bringing the students' work together. There should be a tangible product that will show the students concrete outcomes. It is usually up to the faculty leader to facilitate this.

Although there is no one model for conducting a class using PAR principles just as there is no one way to do PAR (McTaggart, 1997), we simply offer some observations from this particular experience. The very nature of the process requires flexibility: the ability to respond to changing conditions and to move through setbacks. The anthropology/Prodigy research class was just one way in which such a project was developed. Even if the effort is repeated in another visual anthropology class, it is virtually certain that the process and the outcome will be greatly different as circumstances and people change. Anthropologists have long been comfortable with research as a dialectical, nonlinear process. We are also becoming increasingly comfortable with that process happening in dynamic, collaborative teams that involve active community partnerships. We will be doing our students a service if we introduce them to that process from within the classroom, offering challenges, even frustrations, but ultimately a great feeling of accomplishment and reward.

Endnote

1) The "I" in the piece refers to the first author, while "we" represents the collective voice of the three authors. We would also like to acknowledge the major contributions of the other members of the class research team—Sara Dykins Callahan, Charity Kiser, Jody Owens, and Bob Pomeroy—and the support, patience, and vision of Prodigy Director Carolena von Trapp.

References

Adelman, C. (1997). Action research: The problem of participation. In R. McTaggart (Ed.), *Participatory action research: International contexts and consequences* (pp. 79–106). Albany, NY: State University of New York Press.

Austin, D. E. (2003). Community-based collaborative team ethnography: A community-university-agency partnership. *Human Organization, 62*(2), 143–152.

Baena, V. C., Camas, A. M. P., Sotelo, R. M., & Mateos, M. O. (2004). Revealing the hidden: Making anthropological documentaries. In S. Pink, L. Kürti, & A. I. Afonso (Eds.), *Working images: Visual research and representation in ethnography* (pp. 131–146). New York, NY: Routledge.

Erickson, K. C., & Stull, D. (1998). *Doing team ethnography: Warnings and advice.* Thousand Oaks, CA: Sage.

Holland, B. A. (1997). Analyzing institutional commitment to service: A model of key organizational factors. *Michigan Journal of Community Service Learning, 4,* 30–41.

McTaggart, R. (1997). Guiding principles for participatory action research. In R. McTaggart (Ed.). *Participatory action research: International contexts and consequences* (pp. 25–45). Albany, NY: State University of New York Press.

Moriarty, G. (1997). *Taliruni's travellers: An arts worker's view of evaluation* (Social Impact of the Arts Working Paper No. 7). Stroud, U.K.: Comedia.

Newman, T., Curtis, K., & Stephens, J. (2003). Do community-based arts projects result in social gains? A review of the literature. *Community Development Journal, 38*(4), 310–322.

Pink, S. (2004). Applied visual anthropology: Social intervention, visual methodologies, and anthropological theory. *Visual Anthropology Review, 20*(1), 3–16.

Ramaley, J. A. (2001). Why do we engage in engagement? *Metropolitan Universities, 12*(3),13–19.

Collaborative Action Research at Interchange: A U.K. Model

8

David Hall, Irene Hall

This chapter describes and analyzes the experience of implementing community-based action research in two undergraduate sociology departments in higher education institutions in the United Kingdom (the University of Liverpool and Liverpool Hope University) and considers the evidence of the impact of such research on community organizations and students. The chapter begins with a discussion of how a community-based action research module has been developed over the past 14 years and analyzes the participatory nature of the research model. The role of the Interchange charity, a community organization, is explained along with its connection to the European Science Shop movement, which, according to its mission statement, "provides independent, participatory research support in response to concerns experienced by civil society" (European Commission, 2003, p. 18). We conclude with the comments, concerns, and positive experiences voiced by community organizations and students. This is the ultimate test of whether the collaborative action research model in Liverpool is successful or not.

The term voluntary and community organizations (VCOs) is in current use in the U.K. to refer to the range in scale of organizations in the voluntary sector. It is analogous to the nonprofit sector in the U.S. and to nongovernment organizations (NGOs) in Europe. The staff of voluntary organizations is largely paid and increasingly professional, although many organizations also have volunteer workers who perform a variety of tasks. This includes, for instance, working with service users, running campaigns, or, importantly, forming the trustee boards of management. Community organizations generally rely more on volunteers and have lesser amounts of funding, but do have strong connections to the local community.

Community-Based Action Research

At the University of Liverpool a 30-credit double module in applied social research is offered to final-year undergraduates (seniors), as an alternative to a senior thesis. This double module runs across two semesters, from late September to early May, and accounts for one quarter of the students' assessed coursework for the year. Students must have achieved good grades in their second-year (sophomore) research methods courses. This serves as a quality threshold to ensure that the external community partners and supervising tutors can have confidence in the students' research abilities. The community-based action research module involves classroom-based advanced research training and supervision on a weekly basis from tutors as well as fieldwork experience amounting to approximately one day per week.

The students who choose this option tend to see it as an attractive alternative to conducting a more theoretical and library-based dissertation (senior thesis). It provides them with the opportunity to conduct a real-life project for a local community organization producing results designed to be used to benefit the organization's clients. In any year, it has to be admitted that it is always a minority of students who make such a choice. Community-based action research is a demanding, if rewarding, option, and a student's motivation is likely to be instrumental, career and résumé related, and altruistic.

Validation of the community-based action research program within the academic curriculum has meant ensuring that the demands on students are at least equivalent to the dissertation, with similar credit value and comparable assessment. Having to convince faculty colleagues and examiners of the scholarly status of the activity has certainly enhanced the emphasis on transparent assessment procedures with an explicit attention to quality.

There are four specific criteria in the management of the applied research projects that distinguish them from dissertations:

- The intermediary agency (Interchange) is used to provide the contact and information for students, staff, and organizations about research projects.

- A research agreement is negotiated between the voluntary organization, student, and supervisor at the start of the project.

- Students may work in small teams of between two and four or on their own.

- The written end-of-project assessment, equivalent to a dissertation, comprises two elements: the client report on the research and its findings for the voluntary organization, and the reflective report on how the research was done and what the student learned from it for the academic department.

The use of a common client report and separate individual reflective reports provides a means of assessing individual students within a team, with a relative weighting of 70% for the client report and 30% for the reflective report. This balance has stood the test of time, and present practice differs little in these respects from when the projects started in 1991 (Hall & Hall, 1996).

Students initially contact the Interchange coordinator and select research questions from a list of requests for research submitted by local voluntary and community sector nonprofit organizations across the region of Merseyside, which includes Liverpool and the surrounding metropolitan boroughs in the northwest of England.

Often the request from the voluntary organization is for an evaluation of a service that it supplies to members or service users. Students negotiate the topic and the questions to be explored with their organization backed by their supervisor. After concluding a research agreement, they submit a research protocol, which fleshes out the proposed study by adding timescales and dealing in depth with ethical and methodological issues. Typically, students conduct interviews with the stakeholders of a service or administer questionnaires to them about their perceptions of, and satisfaction with, the service. Observation is also used, and this can sometimes be participatory as students may also act as volunteers within an organization.

The ethical scrutiny of applied research is of great importance. Although there is no institutional requirement for ethical review, each project agreement stipulates that the student abide by the ethical guidelines of the British Sociological Association and the practices of the voluntary organization regarding confidentiality and access to service users. Furthermore, as students go off campus for their research, it is a university requirement that the student and the supervisor carry out a risk assessment before the research activity begins, so potential risks can be avoided or minimized. For example, a student conducting research with service users who meet for an evening session should have a safe way to return home after dark, and, where appropriate, organizations have arranged transportation as they would for their own volunteers.

The Liverpool model emphasizes the importance of negotiation in designing and conducting research. Respect is given to the organization's goals and ethos, to the needs of the student researchers, and to the participants in the research. The research is intended to assist the organization in changing its practice. It is not primarily research or evaluation for theory, and it is not research that exploits an organization for data collection or for academic publication without benefit to the organization (Hall & Hall, 2004).

Stringer (1999) has noted that community-based action research seeks to "give voice" to people who have previously been silent research subjects, and this is particularly apparent when service users are consulted about their views and preferences. Typically, whether a voluntary or community organization serves clients in the fields of mental health, homelessness, youth employability, learning difficulties, older persons' activities, hospital volunteering, environmental action, or community regeneration (to take examples of some of the recent groups that have requested action research projects), the student begins with little or no knowledge of the field and has to depend on the knowledge and experience of the practitioners. Part of the negotiation of a project is to ensure that the views of participants—and particularly those of service users—can be incorporated into the research.

Where recommendations are included in the report, students are advised to ground the recommendations in the evidence that has been collected but also to discuss the recommendations with the organization's managers beforehand. This is to avoid springing surprises on the organization and also, more positively, to abide by the ethos of collaborative partnership. Critical or negative issues can also be dealt with verbally in feedback before they emerge in the report. This allows managers the opportunity to set findings in context or to explain actions that may have been taken in the past, but which a short research study has not been able to encompass. As Punch (1998) has argued, such a research process puts a premium on honesty and openness with participants.

How Participatory Can Community-Based Action Research Become?

The Liverpool model does not move as far as participatory action research, which presents a situation where the researcher becomes the facilitator of research undertaken by the participants. This is for two main reasons: The skills for facilitation are likely to be beyond the novice student action researcher, and the time necessary to implement full cycles of participant observation, reflection, and action is unlikely to be available during a two-semester course.

Rather, the approach to action research fits with the stakeholder evaluation model described by Weiss (1998) in which the evaluator:

> engages in a structured effort to learn [the stakeholders'] concerns, their assumptions, their questions, their data needs, their intentions for the evaluation. She seeks to shape the evaluation to answer their questions and meet their priorities, but she remains in charge of the technical research work. (p. 99)

For organizations using the report for fundraising, a common usage, a criterion in the application for funding is often that independent research must be provided as evidence of need. Consequently, project reports are seen as legitimate sources of evidence, which have been produced though partnership, but retain researcher independence.

European Science Shop Movement

The Liverpool practice is similar to the European Science Shop model, first developed in the Netherlands in the 1970s as part of an agenda to open up the universities to the wider community. "Science Shop" is the literal translation of the Dutch Wetenschapswinkel. The term is rather misleading. It is not a shop in the sense of a place where the public can come to buy goods, but rather a mediation center where community requests for information are received and allocated for staff and research student investigation. The term science is also potentially misleading as it translates better as "knowledge." That is, the disciplines may lie outside of the natural sciences and include the social sciences and humanities. Although in the U.K. Research Exchange is more meaningful, the term Science Shop has become established both in the Dutch universities and at the European level through the European Commission. It is now a recognized brand that is used in European projects and in European scientific policy documentation.

Most, but not all, Science Shops have a university base, and the questions raised by the public may lead to the development of new topics in the university curriculum (Hende & Jørgensen, 2001). Citizen groups typically find it difficult to access the type of scientific research that Science Shops can perform as part of public service and that can also lead to academic publications.

One of the functions envisaged by the European Commission in promoting a dialogue between science and society is that of the early-warning system to alert the scientific community to citizens' concerns that are not being met by science as currently practiced. Conversely, Science Shops can help to improve the public image of science, damaged by concerns over, for example, bovine spongiform encephalopathy (mad cow disease) and genetically modified food. It also leads to greater communication with and respect for the public. As in the United States, there is also a concern in some circles to democratize science by not leaving all the policy decisions to experts but also to involve citizens and civil society (European Commission, 2002).

Science Shops, Research Exchanges, and the Liverpool Interchange

Interchange is a registered charity, currently located in the School of Sociology and Social Policy at the University of Liverpool, but formally independent of it. It exists to link voluntary and community sector organizations with student research projects for the benefit of the organizations themselves and of the students. It was created in 1994 as a successor to Merseyside Community Research Exchange (MCRE), which had been established by the authors in 1991 as part of an initiative of research exchanges that were beginning to emerge in the U.K. at the time, with particular success in Manchester. The original funding for the MCRE was through the government-funded Enterprise in Higher Education initiative, which aimed to develop enterprise and business skills in students to make them more employable. Although many social scientists were suspicious of this business-oriented agenda, it did provide an opportunity for expanding real-life experience to the voluntary nonprofit sector, whose organizations were classified as small and medium enterprises (SMEs).

Right from the start, Interchange received support from the three Liverpool universities—Liverpool Hope University, Liverpool John Moores University, and the University of Liverpool—and developed a model of cooperation and sharing resources for the mutual benefit of all partners. In 1995 Interchange won the national Partnership Trust award competition for projects in higher education in the category of "learning through service." The government minister who presented the award to the Interchange chair remarked that the cooperation between universities in the city was particularly noteworthy. This project was the only one being honored that evening that was not based in one institution.

Against a backdrop of previously strident competition among these universities, this small and modest cooperation was a breakthrough. However, as noted later in the discussion on funding, this cross-institutional cooperation has also proved something of an albatross. Often universities have a preference for claiming the credit for and managing and controlling such offices within their individual structures.

The lessons learned from Interchange have had further national recognition. A consortium of the sociology departments at Birmingham University, Liverpool Hope University, and the University of Liverpool was successful in obtaining funding for the Community-Based Learning Teamwork (CoBaLT) Project. This was a government-funded teaching and learning project in higher education running from 1997–2001 to disseminate ideas on community-based learning within sociology departments in England, through a series of workshops, conferences, and a set of videos and workbooks (Hall & Hall, 2002).

Recognition of Community-Based Action Research by Policymakers

The activities of the international Science Shop movement have succeeded in establishing the relevance and importance of community-based action research in Europe. This has worked at a strategic policy level, although individual Science Shops often struggle to secure financial support from their local university managements. The European Commission has offered its support to Science Shops through a number of research projects in the Research Directorate Section for Science and Society, and Science Shops have been written into the European Science and Society Action Plan, as institutions where:

> Science is placed at the service of local communities and non-profit making associations. Hosted by universities or independent, their common feature is that they answer questions from the public, citizens' associations or NGOs on a wide variety of scientific issues. (European Commission, 2002, p. 15)

The European Commission has also produced an explanatory brochure on Science Shops, which features Interchange among others (European Commission, 2003). Staff at Interchange have been partners in three European Commission research projects. The first, INTER-ACTS, was about the experience and expectations of NGOs, universities, and Science Shops on their interaction (Jørgensen, Hall, Hall, Gnaiger, et al., 2004). The second, the International Science Shop Network (ISS-NET), examined an international network for promoting Science Shop cooperation. The third and most recent project, Training and Mentoring of Science Shops (TRAMS), focused on the training and mentoring of new Science Shops. Details can be found on the International Science Shops web site: www.livingknowledge.org.

Using International Support to Develop Regional Policy

The INTERACTS project adapted the European methodology of scenario workshops (www.cordis.lu/easw/home.html) to envisioning how community-university relationships might develop in the future through the mediation of Science Shops. Four groups of participants—voluntary sector practitioners, students and researchers, Science Shop staff, and educational and local government policy makers—participated in workshops run by all seven international partners in their own countries in order to produce visions and plans for the future.

The results of the Liverpool scenario workshop demonstrated a strong wish by U.K. participants for universities to change their focus and be more value led, responding to community needs via open structures and balanced, community-aware curricula. Participants in the workshop felt that Science Shops should act as a trigger for social change, influencing policy and outcomes while recognizing local expertise. They believed that Science Shops should help drive good practice in community-education engagement, which should be happening on all levels of education, from primary to tertiary, as part of developing citizenship.

From these discussions a number of positive points for action and support by all U.K. participants were agreed upon, including the need for a conference, an accessible resource file, and the creation of a small group network in Liverpool. Interchange followed up the workshop with an international conference on Science Shops and the community in December 2003. The venue was provided free of charge by a community partner. Interchange has organized annual community forums for interested voluntary sector organizations to raise awareness of Interchange and research potential. This has resulted in new community-based action research projects. These are being followed with training workshops designed to help community groups formulate research questions and develop their understanding of research methodology. A regular Interchange newsletter is now produced and circulated to existing and potential community partners.

What Are the Issues in the Support of Interchange by the University?

The question of funding for outreach activities such as Interchange, to provide the means for delivering a public benefit through student research, has always been problematic. It is only in the Dutch universities that Science Shops enjoy a good measure of sustained university funding for mediator/research staff posts through the positive support of their Ministry of Education and university boards. Elsewhere the situation is different and the funding streams more ad hoc, although it has to be added that Dutch universities are not immune from financial pressures, and some Science Shops are experiencing budget cuts or nonreplacement of staff.

Part of the thinking behind the registration of Interchange as a charity under U.K. Charity Law was to give it the legal status helpful for applying for support from funding bodies, which can usually allocate money only to registered organizations. This strategy has had limited success, because many of the grants obtainable are relatively small. In nearly all cases, funding bodies are prepared to finance new projects, as start-up or pump-priming activities, but are much less willing to cover regular costs or core funding such as staffing the Interchange coordinator post.

The funding of Interchange has therefore been supplemented by research funds awarded to the academic supervisors, which have enabled the mediation work to exist alongside research on applied research, Science Shops, learning and teaching, and volunteering within the curriculum. Although no unrestricted university funding is available, Interchange has been able to benefit, albeit indirectly, from initiatives for outreach activities by the Higher Education Funding Council for England (the channel through which the Government supports state universities). The first of these was the CoBaLT project, supported by the Government's Fund for the Development of Teaching and Learning in England. More recently some funding has come from the Higher Education Active Community Fund, which promotes volunteering by students, and the Higher Education Innovation Fund, which focuses on outreach to business and the community.

Within the national context, Interchange fits well with the outreach agenda establishing a third mission of universities in addition to teaching and research. A key component of this is the concept of knowledge transfer from universities to business and the community. Community-based action research actually works both ways, bringing the knowledge and experience of community practitioners into the university while addressing their needs for research. In the university context of educating students, Interchange and community-based action research also meet the employability agenda by offering advanced skills development through practical experience of applied research.

However, one difficulty that has emerged in trying to promote Interchange to potential funding providers is its ties to the university and to learning and teaching. Although many funding organizations can see and understand the benefit of applied social research to small and medium voluntary sector organizations—and to the service users and communities that they serve—such organizations also consider that the benefits to students in terms of learning and skills acquisition means that the university itself should be subsidizing this activity. When the competition for funding is with other needy community-based charities, such funding providers find it difficult to justify grants to Interchange, which is wrongly assumed to have university largesse to draw on.

Interchange has survived thus far through the dedication of its members to the ideal of community-based action research as research that makes a difference to the community and through its ability to garner small amounts of resources from a variety of sources. The beauty of community-based action research is that it can truthfully be presented as meeting many needs in learning and teaching, community development, regional social and economic policy, science and society policy, empowering the voluntary sector, knowledge transfer, science communication, skills assists, lifelong learning, work-based learning, and graduate employment. It impacts students and community members. Community-based action research is well placed to take on and benefit from initiatives in all these directions.

What Has Been the Benefit of Community-Based Action Research to Community Groups?

Small-scale research projects have a good chance of producing results that community organizations can use. As Robson (2000) points out in relation to small-scale evaluation, such projects focus on delivery of very specific services, which means that recommendations are more likely to be implemented than those of a large-scale regional/national program, with much greater costs. Certain evaluation models (e.g., Patton, 1997) emphasize that negotiation throughout the life of the project (not just at the start) is crucial for management to take findings and recommendations on board. However, there is not a great deal of evidence in evaluation and applied research literature on whether reports do get used, and, if so, how. As far as the usage of student community-based action research reports was concerned, the knowledge in Liverpool was patchy and anecdotal.

Therefore, the authors managed to use research funding to explore some of the issues of community-based action research usage. Altogether, three surveys have been conducted with community organizations and students, and a high, if unpredictable, level of usage by organizations has been reported. To summarize, a broad distinction can be made between internal and external use, with internal use referring to the report being read and distributed within the organization and external to use by outside agencies. In addition, reports have been used directly, to improve the service along the lines of the report's recommendations, and indirectly, to raise awareness among staff of service users' feelings or to promote staff development (Hall & Hall, 2004).

Additionally, reports have also been used to generate funding for the organization, and, in extreme cases, to enable the organization to continue to provide services. In one case, for example, an organization has used the report to provide evidence for extra paid staff to run a volunteer service within a hospital. Another organization has used the report to back a successful application for a million-pound community arts initiative for minority ethnic residents.

However, funding is not consistently available to conduct long-term evaluation of the usage of the research. The evaluation form that accompanies the report when it is delivered to the community organization can only elicit immediate reaction to the report itself. So, when ongoing surveys are not being conducted, there remains an issue of hidden usage. An example of this came to light when the manager of a community group, which uses local volunteers to befriend families with problems, was interviewed for one of the CoBaLT videos. She explained that when she took up her position she had discovered a student report, unused, in the filing cabinet. She spotted its potential and was able to use the report as evidence for two consecutive funding applications. It was crucial in helping to keep her organization financially afloat. She stated:

When we're writing funding applications, very often the funders want to know, not just the facts and figures of what we do, but also some of the human interest behind it. Because very often large trusts actually want to know what's real about it, rather than just the accountancy report. And we used the quotations and the stories that Liz gave us. (Hall & Hall, 2000b)

The same manager mentioned another unexpected usage: having a student do this kind of research teaches voluntary organizations how to manage a researcher. She added: "It's cheap; it saves a lot of time; and very often work that they would like to do but cannot see any way of getting done, can be done. And they also feel that they are helping the students." (Hall & Hall, 2000a, p. 34)

How Have Students Benefited From Participating in Interchange Projects?

The following extracts come from the reflective reports written by students to discuss their experiences in conducting community-based research.

Reflective Report by Student "Linda"

The asylum seekers interviewed for the purpose of my project were all "hard cases;" that is to say they had had their applications turned down and had therefore also been refused all support by the National Asylum Support Service. The main skills I feel I have gained have been: a knowledge about asylum issues; confidence in interviewing people and dealing with organizations; a knowledge of the voluntary sector; a knowledge of life in my neighborhood; an improved knowledge of world issues; the ability to work on my own initiative; and having to be assertive to get things done. For me, the most important thing that I have gained from doing this project is feeling like I have made a difference to people's lives and given a voice to individuals who would not normally be heard. One interviewee told me that he felt as if his "mind had been freed" after the interview, which sums up how many of the "hard cases" are feeling. . . . Although they know that I could offer no practical help to individuals, they did seem to appreciate that the project would be used by the Law Center to show the hardships of hard cases, and would hopefully help other people like them.

Reflective Report by Student "Diana"

People with learning disabilities often face economic and social exclusion due to incorrect assumptions about their abilities. In contrast MOWL [moving on with learning] seeks to empower the students on the program by providing them with the necessary support and encouragement to develop the skills to think and act independently of their care-providers. As well as learning how to conduct research I also have developed various personal skills as a result of this project that I feel I would have been unable to develop elsewhere in my course. These include the ability to recognize and challenge my own judgmental viewpoints; the confidence and patience to tackle communication difficulties between myself and another person by trying various methods of communication including symbols and pictures; time management and organization skills to ensure the research would be completed by the set date; and report presentation skills. I have also proved to myself that I can effectively deal with problems when they arise and have the necessary skills to produce a report which meets the requirements of the organization.

These comments reveal a positive sense of experience in the face of challenges, and they show evidence of student learning. But the comments also point out some key issues for academics to consider: Should such complexity of understanding be incorporated into the curriculum? Is orthodox, class, and library-based learning, more appropriate for university education?

One way of answering these questions is to listen to the students' voices, such as those whose reflective reports have been excerpted here. Students often comment in these reports on how their experience of working with community groups has enabled them to make connections between abstract concepts learned in the classroom and their application in the world outside. This has enhanced their theoretical learning in sociology and their ability to situate the specific experience of their project within wider social issues. This would surely be seen as appropriate and commendable for a university education by most educators.

Community-based action research can also be linked to relevant best practices discussed in educational literature. For instance, it can be seen as a form of experiential learning (Kolb, 1984), because it promotes learning through a cycle of action and reflection and develops general and transferable skills that are useful in different contexts, particularly in employment.

There is evidence that community-based action research goes beyond employability skills, however, to effecting change in some students' values and priorities. It encourages them to engage in work of "social value," such as service to others, reciprocal learning, and community involvement (Stanton, Giles, & Cruz, 1999). This has certainly been the case with students in Liverpool graduating from the Interchange modules, who, along with community organizations, were interviewed on the surveys already mentioned.

In one survey, 30 former Interchange students who had completed projects between two and nine years previously were interviewed. The survey aimed to explore the students' perceptions and memories of their experience and to discover whether it had affected their subsequent careers. The findings, published elsewhere (Hall & Hall, 2002), are summarized here.

The degree of students' personal engagement with their project was shown when they were asked to recall the highlights. Almost half specifically mentioned the people they had worked with, especially those using the service of the organization studied. Several interviewees used the term hands-on as a contrast to their other university learning. Seven people said the highlight was participating in a project to benefit others, which had given satisfaction and motivation to their work. As one person put it, "I felt I was putting something back into the community" (Hall & Hall, 2002, p. 106). For five people, the practical use of the research was the highlight. "You knew it would be used as a report," one remarked.

Problem solving was a common part of the learning, with only four people reporting no difficulties or "none we didn't overcome" (Hall & Hall, 2002, p. 106). The others listed 35 difficulties, with the largest category concerning difficulties in gaining access to interviewees. A common outcome of such problems was for the research itself to change direction. Time management was also mentioned as a significant problem.

Two-thirds of the sample stated that their project had influenced their career direction, and almost half of these mentioned that it was the research activity that had been influential. For five students, the project encouraged them to enter careers working with people. Skills developed through community-based action research, which were being applied in careers that included improved communication and report writing skills and an ability to plan work "rather than just dive straight in" (Hall & Hall, 2002, p. 107). Improved social awareness was also mentioned, for instance, when teachers were discussing their understanding of pupils' backgrounds.

The last word on student benefit from community-based action research goes to the student who addressed a community forum in

Liverpool. Speaking of his project and what he had learned, he stated to the academic staff and community groups listening:

I thought this is what I would be learning when I came to university, but I found it wasn't like that. It wasn't until I came on this course in my final year that I found what I feel university education should be about. (Morris, 2005, p. 183)

Conclusion

Collaborative action research at Liverpool has been found to have considerable impact—on students and on the community. The European Science Shop movement has provided support for and input into the developments at Interchange, and Interchange has made its mark on the movement as an example of a successful university-based sociology Science Shop. Ultimately the success of the Liverpool initiative depends on the commitment and expertise of all the participants, sharing their time and knowledge to produce research that is beneficial. This type of initiative can continue to flourish, however, only if it receives recognition from individual universities, backed by the support of national government policy and funding programs that enable students to learn in the wider community—in the not-for-profit sector as well as in the business world. The European Science Shops show that participation in collaborative action research is a profound learning experience and that student researchers from a wide variety of disciplines have a substantial contribution to make to their societies.

References

European Commission. (2002). *Science and society—Action plan.* Luxembourg, Belgium: Office for Official Communications of the European Communities.

European Commission. (2003). *Science shops—Knowledge for the community* (EUR 20877). Luxembourg, Belgium: Office for Official Communications of the European Communities.

Hall, D., & Hall, I. (1996). *Practical social research: Project work in the community.* Basingstoke, U.K.: Palgrave Macmillan.

Hall D,. & Hall I. (2000a). *Embedding community based research in academic teaching and learning through evaluation.* Paper presented to the U.K. Evaluation Society Conference, London, U.K.

Hall I., & Hall D. (2000b). *Researching in the community: A positive partnership.* Liverpool, U.K.: Workbook 2, CoBaLT Project, University of Liverpool, Department of Sociology.

Hall I., & Hall, D. (2002). Incorporating change through reflection: Community based learning. In R. Macdonald & J. Wisdom (Eds.), *Academic and educational development: Research, evaluation, and changing practice in higher education* (pp. 105–108). London, U.K.: Kogan Page.

Hall I., & Hall D. (2004). *Evaluation and social research: Introducing small-scale practice.* New York, NY: Palgrave Macmillan.

Hende, M., & Jørgensen, M. (2001). *The impact of Science Shops on university curricula and research* (Scipas Rep. No. 6). Utrecht, Netherlands: University of Utrecht, Science Shop for Biology.

Jørgensen, M. S., Hall, I., Hall, D., Gnaiger, A., et al. (2004). *Democratic governance through interaction between NGOs, universities, and Science Shops: Experiences, expectations, recommendations.* Lyngby, Denmark: The Science Shop, Technical University of Denmark.

Kolb, D. A. (1984). *Experiential learning: Experience as the source of learning and development.* Englewood Cliffs, NJ: Prentice-Hall.

Morris, R. (2005). *Student presentation, Interchange community forum.* Liverpool, U.K.: Interchange, University of Liverpool.

Patton, M. Q. (1997). *Utilization-focused evaluation: The new century text.* Thousand Oaks, CA: Sage.

Punch, M. (1998). Politics and ethics in qualitative research. In N. K. Denzin & Y. S. Lincoln (Eds.), *The landscape of qualitative research: Theories and issues* (pp. 156–184). Thousand Oaks, CA: Sage.

Robson, C. (2000). *Small-scale evaluation: Principles and practice.* London, U.K.: Sage Publications.

Stanton, T., Giles, D., & Cruz, N. (1999). *Service-learning: A movement's pioneers reflect on its origins, practice, and future.* San Francisco, CA: Jossey-Bass.

Stringer, E. T. (1999). *Action research: A handbook for practitioners* (2nd ed.). Thousand Oaks, CA: Sage.

Weiss, C. H. (1998). *Evaluation: Methods for studying programs and policies* (2nd ed.). Upper Saddle River, NJ: Prentice-Hall.

Checks and Balances: The Aftermath of Course-Based Action Research

9

Nila Ginger Hofman

Our contributors have examined the ways in which course-based action research (CBAR) differs from more traditional undergraduate courses. We have emphasized that CBAR includes and goes beyond the civic engagement promised in service-learning and strictly student-centered research, because it implements projects that, by embracing a critical pedagogy, are for and with community partners.[1] Although as educators and academic officers our primary responsibilities are to our students, community-based projects are not envisioned as testing grounds in which students can hone their ethnographic research skills or acquire experience with, for example, GIS mapping. Instead, CBAR projects seek, in the first instance, to empower local community-based organizations and their stakeholders. Many of us have advocated for a different approach to educating and conducting research—one that focuses on the confluence of teaching, research, and activism. This is best articulated by Beth Catlett and Irene Beck in Chapter 2, where they emphasize that CBAR is about "reinforcing synergies between research, teaching, and community engagement."

What has also become clear through the contributions to this volume is that relatively few social scientists have been engaged in CBAR. Some have argued that this is due to a lack of institutional support. Indeed, it takes more than the willingness of individual faculty to incorporate

CBAR. The unique characteristics of universities such as DePaul University, Chicago State University, Cornell University, and a number of universities in Liverpool, U.K., and elsewhere is that they have had an enormous impact on helping faculty to develop progressive CBAR. But faculty can and should do more than this. DePaul's unique climate helps facilitate CBAR through programs such as the Irwin W. Steans Center for Community-Based Service-learning. This is emphasized in Chapter 5 by Winifred Curran, Euan Hague, and Harpreet Gill, who note that DePaul finds itself an active participant in the social politics of students' experiences. In Chapter 1, Howard Rosing, the executive director of the center, echoes this same point by noting that the center provides support to faculty, community organizations, and students through opportunities grounded in Vincentian values. In contrast, David Hall and Irene Hall point out in Chapter 8 that many universities are either unable to fund CBAR projects, or the projects turn out to be too costly to maintain.

Due to a lack of support for CBAR, the impact of student-driven research on community partners has been left largely unaddressed. Our contributors describe many of the successes of CBAR for their students, but none directly question the nature of the impact that CBAR has had on community participation in the aftermath of CBAR. Much like the CBAR project described by Elizabeth Bird, Jess Paul Ambiee, and James Kuzin in Chapter 7, this chapter includes a number of smaller CBAR projects that are worthy of postresearch examination. My aim is to help fill this gap by considering the after effects of CBAR on three participating community partners in and around Chicago, long after student researchers have left the field sites.

I pursue this aim by drawing on a series of follow-up interviews with community-based organization (CBO) representatives, which position the projects in the context of an anthropological research paradigm. In order to further explore some of the topics already discussed in previous chapters, I chose to include projects designed around the needs of a small-business-development organization that combats gentrification, an organization that offers a range of services to noncitizens including citizenship exam preparation classes, and an organization that assists noncitizens in filing applications for immigration benefits.

CBAR, Service-Learning, and Anthropology

While service-learning programs are rapidly developing in universities across the nation, action research, which promotes research leading to social justice, lags behind (McNicoll, 1999). The variety of CBAR approaches employ similar pedagogical tools for engaging students in goal-oriented research that is designed in cooperation with the participating CBOs. The central difference between action research and the more popular service-learning is that service-learning focuses on providing a service, which includes but is not confined to research endeavors, while action research focuses on achieving social change. Action research—aptly described by Howard Rosing in Chapter 1—ideally incorporates a critical pedagogical approach that challenges students' existing values and moves them from a familiar social and psychological location to one he rightfully describes as "uncomfortable." This became particularly meaningful to me when I attended a symposium in Chicago on service-learning to which almost no community partners were invited. In his opening address, the president of the university said that higher education is increasingly envisioned as a private, not a public, good. Individual students are thus its primary targets.

As educators and academic officers, we are all too familiar with Savio—who rose to prominence in the 1960s as the leader of Berkeley's Free Speech Movement—and his gripping metaphor of the university as a factory, where students are primed to become "well-behaved citizens" and where faculty are mere cogs in the machine that perpetuates an intellectual and moral wasteland. Reminiscent of Savio's metaphor, the academy in the new millennium is now a corporate business: Its students are consumers, and the faculty is its principal commodity. In this light, approaches to teaching that are described as student centered and service-learning—which promises to present real-life scenarios without challenging students' comfort zones—are intended merely to boost consumer satisfaction. Like the production of neo-liberal citizens described by Hyatt (2001), students seek the thrill of authentic urban adventures, which even well-intentioned programs risk inadvertently providing.

A less pessimistic view of service-learning sees the success of service-learning programs as resulting from efforts to "recast the university as a publicly engaged institution" (Boyer, 1990, p. 138). This is certainly true of urban universities, such as DePaul, that acknowledge the need to become more engaged with their communities. Responding to this need, many such programs promote civic responsibility and selflessness by providing practical assistance to communities and charitable organizations (Ferrari & Chapman, 1999) while also expanding innovative educational opportunities for students.

Although only a few anthropologists have employed service-learning—there are fewer anthropology departments across the nation than service-learning programs—even fewer have incorporated action research into their courses (O'Donnell, 2003; Schensul, Berg, Schensul, & Sydkim, 2004; Simonelli, 2000; Simonelli & Roberts, 1998). Part of the reason for this, as Keith Morton (1995) has pointed out, is that if students are not sufficiently prepared for research, student-driven service or action research risks hurting CBOs by reinforcing negative stereotypes. This is an issue of concern for anthropologists and other social scientists who are thinking about incorporating CBAR in undergraduate courses. Another issue, which Howard Rosing addresses, is that student-centered action research requires significant amounts of planning and preparation. Accordingly, lack of support for faculty interested in developing CBAR (e.g., in terms of time allocation, research staff, and funding as well as a lack of undergraduate students' exposure to research methods, professionalism, ethics, and analysis) is why many anthropologists have not yet incorporated CBAR into their courses.

Lack of funding and support for faculty is not only an issue in the U.S. As David Hall and Irene Hall point out in Chapter 8, Dutch universities, for example, enjoy a certain amount of sustained funding for CBAR projects, but they are not immune to financial pressures. This has also proven to be true for universities in Liverpool, U.K., where generally more institutional support for CBAR exists than in the U.S.

A special issue of the Michigan Journal of Community Service Learning published in 2004, titled "Service-Learning and Anthropology," addresses the lack of anthropologists' engagement in CBAR in the U.S. This much-needed voice in the discussion of the role of local community-based research and teaching anthropology focuses on the impact of community-based research on students' learning. In doing so, it initiates a long-overdue dialogue about the relationship between student researchers and those the research is aimed to serve. Of particular importance is the notion that incorporating participatory action research into community-based courses could help mitigate problems associated with student-driven research by reshaping the role of the "expert anthropologist" in terms of the reflective and collaborative dialogue in which faculty and student researchers work together to promote the empowerment of communities and their stakeholders. This approach attempts to bridge the community-university divide by recasting the university as a public good. Rather than treating students as consumerist subjects—who are never required to challenge their value systems or leave their comfort zones—this approach envisions the university as an institution capable of evincing a genuine commitment to preparing students for the lifelong project of pursuing solutions to local and global inequalities.

Pedagogies of Social Change and Action

How does one teach community-based action research to undergraduate students? Tenure-track assistant professors at liberal arts colleges face a number of challenges in this regard. CBAR projects take great effort to design and monitor. From colleagues who participated at the Urban Research and Curriculum Transformation Institute (in summer, 2003) organized by the Field Museum in Chicago, I learned that course-based research projects are most rewarding for students and useful to stakeholders when instructors themselves are engaged in the field project. This can be achieved by frequent site visitation and long-term projects in which faculty conduct research along with student researchers. Differently put, social science scholars teach by sharing their professional experiences with students and by active participation in the research project. However, not all institutions of higher education are open to having their faculty conduct research primarily designed with the goals of CBOs and teaching in mind. In addition, there are often a variety of reasons why faculty members are unable to sustain long-term research projects involving student coresearchers, community partners, and their stakeholders.

Another challenge is undergraduate students' research skills and field-work experience. A successful CBAR project has prerequisites for students enrolled in the course. In anthropology, students ideally will have already completed a course on (ethnographic) research methods and ethics and have had some ethnographic field research experience prior to enrolling in a CBAR course. As McNicoll (1999) observes, incorporating action-oriented research into university courses raises a number of potential obstacles, including implementing a new perspective on teaching, research, and students' work evaluation. Working under time constraints is another significant challenge faced by faculty when designing CBAR courses. As Elizabeth Bird, Jess Paul Ambiee, and James Kuzin indicate (see Chapter 7), the question remains: How effective are CBAR projects that are confined to one semester (typically 16 weeks) or an even a shorter time span of one quarter (ten weeks)?

That said, it is likely that students are going to gain from CBAR projects no matter what the direct outcome of their experiences. However, teaching action research is most effective if students are involved in a research project that is designed in cooperation with the participating CBO and are advised that doing action-based ethnography is often frustrating (particularly if the course is only ten weeks long). Students should also be cautioned that participatory action research does not come without obstacles and that it can best be seen as an ongoing and emergent process rather than a social research method that presumes equal power-sharing among research partners (Maguire, 1993). Because full-scale collaboration with the participating CBOs is often not possible (or, in some cases, not desirable), I embrace the view that collaboration with CBOs should be viewed as an evolving ideal (Greenwood, Foote Whyte, & Harkavy, 1993). The focus in CBAR is therefore on developing pedagogies that help facilitate social change, CBO empowerment, and student understanding rather than the older understanding of participatory research offered by William Foote Whyte (1991) in which study participants actively partake in the design, data collection, and dissemination of the research study.

Methodology

In the three projects I discuss here, student researchers used ethnographic data collection as the basis for offering recommendations to CBOs on how better to serve their clients and positively affect stakeholders. The students were upper-level anthropology majors with anthropological research experience. In order to save time, the research objectives were designed in dialogue with the CBOs prior to the beginning of the course. In light of the research objectives, students were asked to produce a report detailing their research findings and analyses.

The fieldwork component for the courses was significant. Students were required to spend a minimum of four hours per week in the field in addition to attending three hours of class per week. The required reading was subject specific and the writing requirements were correspondingly subject focused. Students maintained a field journal in which they documented their research experiences. These were evaluated on a weekly basis. Student-produced field notes were shared periodically with the class (via Blackboard technology) and later used as data in their final reports and research papers.

Students documented the interactions with CBO staff and their clients through participant observation, casual conversations, and open-ended interviews. Participant observation was also employed at different community events and in the neighborhoods of the participating CBOs. Participant observation and interviews were collected over an eight-week period, in either the autumn (September through October) or winter (January through February) quarter. Most interviews were conducted at the participating CBOs, sometimes with the use of Spanish-language interpreters, provided either by the Steans Center or selected from the pool of bilingual students enrolled in the course. In other instances, CBO staff functioned as translators.

Visions for Social Change

Students conducted research for a course titled Visions for Social Change (in 2002), my first community-based action research course (see Howard Rosing's description of this pilot CBAR project in Chapter 1). Eight students conducted research in several CBOs in Humboldt Park of Chicago, including the Division Street Business District Association (DSBDA), a local, community-based business development organization where three students were placed. These students addressed the social, economic, and political issues faced by Humboldt Park residents through the analysis of taped interviews from neighborhood residents and business owners. Their interviews focused on the establishment of a Paseo Boricua, or a Puerto Rican Town, much in the spirit of Chicago's Chinatown business district. From the perspective of DSBDA, the establishment of a Paseo Boricua was envisioned as a way for Humboldt Park neighborhood residents and business owners (as well as the wider Chicagoland Puerto Rican community) to appropriate gentrification efforts that were beginning to emerge in neighboring communities to the east and northeast of Humboldt Park. DSBDA requested that taped interviews be collected from select neighborhood residents whom they identified and Puerto Ricans who had moved out of the neighborhood.

Students suggested that displacement and gentrification might be mitigated by promoting Humboldt Park as a cultural resource for all residents of this community, cleaning up the street and storefronts by adding planters and facades, establishing stores that serve existing community members and creating a sidewalk atmosphere that embraces the ethnic diversity of the community. Their recommendations included proposals for community beautification projects through the utilization of signage and architectural images on Division Street (the commercial strip). Based on interviews with non-Puerto Rican residents, students pointed out that although Humboldt Park is a multicultural community, the existing Paseo Boricua concept did little to acknowledge the diversity of its residents. They further noted that some community residents found the idea of Paseo Boricua to be culturally exclusivist. Some study participants feared that Paseo Boricua would ultimately displace residents and also fail to guarantee the return of Puerto Ricans to the Humboldt Park community.

I spoke with Enrique Salgado, the executive director of DSBDA, about the students' research and recommendations. The overall feeling about student recommendations was positive. However, Salgado pointed out that he felt that the research had been mostly about "reeducating students' biases and exposing them to cultural diversity in the city than about anything else" (personal communication, March–April, 2005). This notwithstanding, DSBDA much appreciated the taped interviews, which provided an oral history of the neighborhood. What DSBDA took away from the project was the need to establish a medium through which community input about Paseo Boricua could be communicated. DSBDA said that they had fortified neighborhood beautification campaigns and made the existing storefronts more attractive based on students' recommendations. They helped realize a number of businesses that continue to serve existing community members since the students' research, including an art gallery that represents Puerto Rican artists, a restaurant serving Puerto Rican cuisine, and a diner-style restaurant/cafe. However, DSBDA did not recognize the need to establish stores or create an atmosphere that could potentially embrace the ethnic diversity in Humboldt Park.

Another highlight of student research was the need to establish intercultural communication. In 2004 a bilingual community newspaper, La Voz del Paseo Boricua, was published. The newspaper details all matters concerning the community, thereby being more inclusive. However, as its name indicates, La Voz del Paseo Boricua focuses not exclusively but predominantly on the Puerto Rican contingent in Humboldt Park. Students' suggestions about the need for beautification projects proved more useful. Together with other CBOs, DSBDA helped establish a prominent mural by a local Puerto Rican artist and implemented a façade program that has been responsible for the frontage of eight stores on the commercial strip, including the art gallery, two restaurants, and a dance school.

Seeking U.S. Citizenship

Eight students conducted research for a course titled International Applied Practice: Seeking U.S. American Citizenship in the Age of Globalization and International Terrorism (in 2003). Two out of eight students conducted research in citizenship exam classes offered at the Albany Park Community Center (APCC). Generally, students sought to better understand how citizenship exam takers negotiate the pressures of becoming naturalized in a political economy described as increasingly hostile toward legal permanent residents (previously called resident aliens), new immigrants, and refugees. Through their research, they addressed a variety of issues, including the cultural underpinnings of the naturalization process, the lived experiences and goals of citizenship seekers, and the sociopolitical issues that affect citizenship exam programs at Chicago-based CBOs. On a more practical level, students' recommendations focused on the effectiveness of programs designed to service citizenship seekers and the ways in which the programs might potentially be improved.

The recommendations students made to APCC included incorporating English as a second language (ESL) instruction with citizenship exam classes, creating a special training or workshop for citizenship exam program volunteers, and creating a special training or workshop for citizenship seekers who felt poorly prepared for dealing with nervousness prior to the exam.

The first recommendation (incorporating ESL with the citizenship exam classes) was due largely to the observation that citizenship seekers memorized potential exam questions and claimed that they "felt at a loss" or "were tricked into" having to answer questions that varied slightly from the ones they had studied for. Students noted that ESL was not only important for passing the citizenship exam but for general life skills and that ESL would help increase noncitizens' potential for achieving upward mobility, independence, and success in the U.S.

In the second recommendation, students described feeling ill prepared for volunteering in the citizenship exam program and recommended that a special training or workshop be created for volunteers offering their services in the program. Based on their observation that citizenship seekers felt nervous prior to the exam, students recommended that a special workshop be incorporated into the program addressing how best to deal with, or alleviate, the apprehensions of exam takers. Students noted that although citizenship seekers studied for both the oral and written components of the exam, they were much more apprehensive about the oral part.

I spoke with Becky Keane, the adult education and citizenship coordinator at APCC about the students' recommendations. She pointed out that a number of recommendations have been incorporated into the citizenship exam program at APCC, including incorporating ESL as part of the citizenship exam package, training volunteers to work in the citizenship exam program, and adding a discussion on how to prepare for the citizenship exam interview. Keane helped to design the research objectives and had been in close contact with the students offering their services at APCC. One of the students, an anthropology senior, was offered a full-time position at APCC soon after she graduated.

Keane explained that although APCC was aware of the importance of ESL to citizenship seekers, APCC had not really started to encourage the exam takers to take ESL classes prior to receiving the recommendations that it should do so. She pointed out that the social and financial responsibilities faced by citizenship seekers continue to be the main obstacles preventing citizenship seekers (especially women) from taking ESL classes. Although a marked 30% increase was noted among the citizenship exam preparation pool, APCC was not in the position to require ESL of citizenship exam takers, primarily for fear of turning people away.

Based on concerns expressed by students, APCC created a citizenship exam program volunteer orientation workshop that required prospective volunteers to take two online courses: Citizenship–Teaching U.S. Civics for the Exam and Citizenship: What Volunteers Need to Know. According to Keane, the workshop provides generous information about the lives of citizenship exam takers, addresses citizen application procedures, and provides learning materials for volunteers.

Finally, although APCC did not organize a separate workshop for addressing exam takers' nervousness, they did create a handout detailing how best to prepare for the exam and interview, including what to wear and bring to the interview, and how best to compose oneself before and during the interview.

Cracking Down on Fraudulent Immigration Counseling

Thirteen students conducted research for a course titled Partners in Action Research: Cracking Down on Fraudulent Immigration Counseling in Kane County, Illinois (in 2004). All 13 students' research was focused on addressing the fraudulent immigration counseling problem, more specifically on the ways in which Centro de Información (Centro) might better promote its expertise and encourage noncitizens to obtain legal services from qualified immigration consultants. Students addressed these problems by documenting and comparing the experiences of noncitizens with fraudulent immigration counseling in two different CBO locations in Chicagoland: Centro and Pueblo Sin Fronteras legal aid office. The rationale behind adding another CBO field site was that there were not enough study participants to accommodate all the students.

Students offered a comparative analysis of the locations and the social relations embedded in them and made a number of recommendations to Centro, including incorporating community outreach and peer education, adjusting the CBO space to a more home-like feel, and seeking supplementary support for staff.

Students recommended that Centro warn noncitizens about immigration fraud through community outreach and peer-education efforts. They suggested that a community outreach-liaison from Centro be appointed and that the discussion panels be led by testimonials from noncitizens who have had harmful interactions with nonaccredited counselors. Students envisioned the latter approach to be the most powerful means for spreading information about fraudulent counseling and advertising accredited immigration counseling services, in part because it could be achieved through the same informal (i.e., word-of-mouth) networks through which nonaccredited counselors operate.

Students pointed out that in order for patrons to seek out accredited counselors, they must feel comfortable in the space where they go to seek counseling. They pointed out that fraudulent counselors provide such a place, while Centro's space, by contrast, felt too office like and sterile. They recommended adjusting Centro's space in such a manner that noncitizens would feel more comfortable going there. They noted that Centro needed to ease the minds of its patrons and reaffirm that they were in a safe environment. Here is how one student put it:

In contrast to Centro, Pueblo Sin Fronteras has a more comfortable atmosphere due to its home-like structure and layout, in addition to a very laid back environment that is family friendly (children were allowed to wander around freely, there was entertainment provided). From my experience visiting Centro, there is an almost sterile feeling that conjures up the stereotypical idea of "office life." There are large open spaces, such as in the entry to the office section that is underused, with only a couple of sitting chairs and one small table. This area at Centro could be used for practical purposes.

The quality of service observed at Centro was based on attitudes of indifference among the staff. Students pointed out that CBOs do not pay their staff as much as they might earn in the private sector and that the limited funds allocated to CBO employees often led to overworked and underpaid employees with low motivation levels. Recommendations ranged from seeking supplemental funding to building a network of volunteers and peer educators who could help immigration consultants with clerical work and other administrative matters.

I spoke with Rodney Fitzgerald (a former immigration and naturalization consultant who worked at Centro at the time of the student research), Rosa Sanborn, and Audrey Ramos (the executive director of Centro who read the students' reports). Fitzgerald, with whom I had coordinated the research project, and Sanborn expressed concern about Centro being understaffed. Since the time of the research, Centro has downscaled from four to two immigration and naturalization consultants. Sanborn said that she felt overwhelmed by the amount of work for which she and the rest of the staff were responsible, and said that clients had to wait up to two weeks for an appointment with an immigration counselor. She claimed that the fact that no new services had been added since the students' research a year before our conversation was a direct result of the budget cuts. On a more promising note, Sanborn said that she had become the community outreach coordinator. Although she had come to recognize the need for peer education efforts, she lacked the time to take the additional responsibilities. Sanborn and Fitzgerald described students' recommendations to give the interior of Centro a more home-like feel as naive, although they were not offended by the recommendations.

Ramos's response to the student recommendations was very different from that of Sanborn and Fitzgerald. Although Ramos had been aware that Fitzgerald and I had discussed the research project at great length before and after the course had ended, she had no substantive knowledge of the project prior to reading the students' reports. Ramos said that she was outraged by student observations. She described feeling insulted about the sterile-feel description of Centro and the negative comparison to Sin Fronteras. She said that her organization takes great pride in being housed in such an environment and that they did not want to portray a "backwards" image. She declined to comment on the cutbacks (she did not care to discuss Centro's financial matters with me) and attitudes of indifference among staff observed by the students. She said that community outreach efforts were already in progress before the student research project and that she did not believe that peer education would help Centro's cause.

Discussion

CBAR provides anthropology students with an opportunity to serve CBOs directly. It also provides them with the experience of being involved in a research project that in many instances leads to the direct implementation of their recommendations. As a result of their research, students were able to evaluate their findings critically and offer useful recommendations to the participating CBOs.

The three examples illustrate that CBAR works best not only when classes are smaller—a factor instructors cannot always control—but when fewer students conduct research at one particular organization. Although the Cracking Down on Fraudulent Immigration Counseling course had only 13 students, it was more difficult to manage than the other two courses, because all 13 students conducted research at the same organization. This put pressure on the participating CBO and on students having to share study participants for interviews. Although Centro agreed to the addition of another CBO site in order to accommodate student research efforts, in the end it was perceived as threatening to Centro's identity.

The foregoing examples illustrate that CBAR works best when contact is sought and maintained with all members of the participating CBOs, and when the different phases of the student research efforts are being communicated throughout the duration of the project. Even though all projects were conceived as a result of conversations with the participating CBOs, some CBOs were more involved with the course project than others. The latter scenario resulted in students checking in more frequently with CBO representatives during the course of their research and establishing a richer communication with the CBOs.

The Seeking U.S. American Citizenship project was successful, because communication with the participating CBO was maintained throughout the project, and students provided what was perceived as a useful service—teaching—to the CBO in addition to their research-based recommendations. The project was also successful, because the CBO was familiar with the nature of anthropological research and did not view the student recommendations as a personal affront or threat to the CBO's identity.

The Visions for Social Change project—in which students produced a critical analysis of their findings and went well beyond the original, more narrowly defined, research objectives—was not as well received. The participating CBO was somewhat taken aback by the student recommendations, because communication with the CBO was limited to the beginning and end of the project and because the limits of students' research were not sufficiently communicated. Here again, the student recommendations were in some ways not well received, because they appeared to threaten the existing status quo of the organization.

Similarly, problems arose when communication about the project was not maintained with all members of the participating CBOs. The Cracking Down on Fraudulent Immigration Counseling project illustrates this point most clearly. Ramos, in this instance, reacted negatively to students' recommendations, including the benign suggestion that peer education efforts should be implemented for the purpose of community outreach. She had not been involved with the conceptualization of the research and had no interaction with the staff (who had knowledge of the project), the students, or the faculty. Ramos was also unfamiliar with the purpose of social science research in general and anthropological analysis in particular.

Among the three projects outlined in this chapter, the best outcome of CBAR is when it is combined with a direct service and when participating CBOs are able to view student-produced research as a valuable service to their organizations and communities. The real strength of implementing sustained communication efforts with CBOs, including an explanation of the limits of student-produced research and the nature of applied anthropological inquiry and analysis, is that this could help move CBAR toward greater community participation. This would certainly help ease the perception of the "expert anthropologist" role and CBOs' feelings of vulnerability regarding student recommendations.

Concluding Thoughts

Pedagogies of Praxis examines the collaboration among faculty, students, and community partners. Through our case studies, we address action-based research pedagogies for the purpose of empowering and advocating for local communities while educating our students. We use CBAR as an umbrella term to explore a number of different approaches—including those we call asset based and feminist informed—to reach our shared goal of improving the lives of those in marginalized communities, to teach and learn to enact genuine social change, and to bridge the community-university divide.

Designing CBAR has proven particularly difficult for untenured faculty, many of whom have taken significant career risks in order to commit extra time to develop and sustain CBAR projects. However, as the contributions to this book demonstrate, universities across the U.S. and elsewhere are starting to acknowledge the benefits of CBAR—some for the purpose of broadcasting themselves as publicly engaged institutions, others to support faculty in their research endeavors and prepare students for the future. Many departments at DePaul, including the one where I work, have started to take into account unrefereed or unpublished work, as part of individual faculty members' records for promotion and tenure. This enables junior faculty to embrace CBAR as part of their scholarship and teaching trajectory. Adopting this approach makes sense for universities that consider good scholarship and teaching to be interrelated. The anthropology department at DePaul regards unpublished study reports as serving the needs of the community and thus as a record of productive scholarship. Furthermore, the department acknowledges that, for faculty who do applied research, these study reports constitute the primary record of research.

Some contributors have stressed that collaborative action research has positively impacted student learning and community partners (Chapters 3, 4, 5, and 8, are all good examples). Others have pointed out the frustration of students, community partners, and faculty due to the demanding workload and the difficulty of working for progressive social change in the face of institutions designed to resist it. The negotiation of collaborative team dynamics continues to present challenges to CBAR, as does the attempt to erase the community-university divide by working with undergraduate students who often are privileged and thus relatively isolated from the social and economic realities outside of the socioeconomic context in which they were raised.

As Daniel Block and Mark Bouman point out in Chapter 6, involving graduate students in CBAR generally assisted the undergraduate learning experience and boosted academic rigor. Their case study illustrates that a number of divides can be bridged through CBAR, including the formation of so-called educational pipelines in which different levels of students can be integrated in a project. This nonhierarchical and noncompetitive approach is also reflected in the feminist-informed model set forth by Beth Catlett and Irene Beck in Chapter 2. Indeed, Catlett and Beck poignantly observe that accommodating different levels of student preparation is necessary if faculty members are to remain committed to meeting the challenges of "ensuring a successful educational experience for students and of developing a research project that upholds high quality and rigorous scientific standards." Such an approach is necessary if we are to take seriously the impact our students might have on the welfare of future generations and if we are to remain committed to empowering our community partners through CBAR.

Emphasizing a different type of academic rigor—one that takes researchers' positionality seriously—helps dispel the myth of the rational, disinterested social scientist whose aim is to distance himself emotionally from the study at hand in order to secure objectivity. In Chapter 7 Elizabeth Bird, Jess Paul Ambiee, and James Kuzin caution that mandatory debriefings, discussions, and self-reflection sessions are necessary for securing successful CBAR projects. Howard Rosing's case study (Chapter 1) best illustrates CBAR's potential for boosting students' critical understanding of social issues, including their relative privilege. Students are encouraged to reach an understanding of their own privilege through reflection, keeping a field diary and forming meaningful, and at times life-altering, relationships.

We have also seen a variety of problems that may arise when community partners are not debriefed or otherwise included in the conceptualization of CBAR. For example, CBOs that are excluded in these ways often develop unrealistic expectations of student-driven projects, such as viewing faculty members involved in CBAR as specifically obligated to them because of a general misunderstanding of the relationship between faculty and the limits on university funds available to them.

Finally, the very heart of CBAR—to narrow the university-community divide, and boost student learning through critical pedagogies—is ultimately successful only when projects are designed in collaboration with local community partners. Community partners are right to view universities as obligated to them. This is particularly evident in cases, such as those described in Chapters 5 and 6, where the university is directly responsible for the gentrification that displaces community members. But the nature and scope of these obligations must be clarified to the community partners themselves and to the universities. If faculty members are not able to do this, it is often the result of limits on the resources available to them, which are needed to maintain CBAR projects. This is not to suggest that community partners must be versed in the bureaucratic nuances of obtaining university resources in a climate where CBAR programs are notoriously underfunded. However, faculty obligations to community partners are discharged, in part, by including community partners in the conceptualization of CBAR. This requires an ongoing dialogue about the nature and limits of the university's obligations to community partners and about faculty members' limited ability to influence the fiscal policies of their employers. In this connection, the future of CBAR depends in large part on the support from institutions of higher education needed to fund programs that will enable students to continue to serve and learn in the wider community and to permit faculty to engage in CBAR without jeopardizing their careers.

In sum, CBAR is a burgeoning and promising addition to the social science curriculum, the future of which depends on a nuanced and critical approach to thinking about the complex interrelationship among its primary stakeholders: institutions of higher learning, faculty members and students, and community partners. Of course, this is not only a matter of theorizing the nature and limits of these constituencies. Rather, in the first instance, it is about the practical work of ensuring that no one is left out of the conversation. As the contributions to this volume illustrate, the array of institutionalized obstacles that stand against CBAR, or any program that challenges the norms of civic responsibility, requires that faculty engaged in CBAR continue to take an improvisational approach to keeping the conversation going.

Endnote

1) Although service-learning has meanings for different audiences—for example, our contributors emphasize collaboration with community partners, activism, and social change—the most popular meaning is linked to student learning and civic engagement.

References

Boyer, E. L. (1990). *Scholarship reconsidered: Priorities of the professoriate.* Princeton, NJ: Carnegie Foundation for the Advancement of Teaching.

Ferrari, J. R., & Chapman, J. G. (1999). Educating students to make-a-difference: Community-based service learning. *Journal of Prevention & Intervention in the Community, 18*(1/2), 5–23.

Foote Whyte, W. (Ed.). (1991). *Participatory action research.* London, U.K.: Sage Publications.

Greenwood, D. J., Foote Whyte, W., & Harkavy, I. (1993). Participatory action research as a process and as a goal. *Human Relations, 46*(2),175–192.

Hyatt, S. B., (2001) 'Service learning,' applied anthropology and the production of neo-liberal citizens. *Anthropology in Action, 8*(1), 6–13.

Maguire, P. (1993). Challenges, contradictions and celebrations: Attempting participatory research as a doctoral student. In P. Part, M. Bryden-Miller, B. Hall, & T. Jackson (Eds.), *Voices of change: Participatory research in the United States and Canada* (pp. 157–176). Westport, CT: Bergin & Garvey.

McNicoll, P. (1999). Issues in teaching participatory action research. *Journal of Social Work, 35*(1), 51–62.

Morton, K. (1995). The irony of service: Charity, project, and social change in service-learning. *Michigan Journal of Community Service Learning, 2*, 19–32.

O'Donnell, K. (2003). Rural teens and communities confront the roots of adolescent pregnancy: The promise of project research. *Practicing Anthropology, 25*(4), 23–36.

Schensul, J. J., Berg, M., Schensul, D., & Sydkim, S. (2004). Core elements of participatory action research for educational empowerment and risk prevention with urban youth. *Practicing Anthropology, 26*(2), 5–9.

Simonelli, J. (2000). Field school in Chiapas. *Qualitative Inquiry,* 6(1),104–106.

Simonelli, J., & Roberts, B. (1998). Connecting classroom with community: Service and professional socialization in applied programs for undergraduates. *Practicing Anthropology, 20*(4), 45–48.

INDEX